Jean,
Thank you! This
being on this
of life together.
Love
Deborah 11.11.16

SILENCE

DEBORAH RAVENWOOD

BALBOA.
PRESS
A DIVISION OF HAY HOUSE

Copyright © 2016 Deborah Ravenwood.
Photo of Author by David Edgecomb
Cover Photo by Kymberli Anne Ravenwood Goldsmith

All rights reserved. No part of this book may be used or reproduced by any means, graphic, electronic, or mechanical, including photocopying, recording, taping or by any information storage retrieval system without the written permission of the author except in the case of brief quotations embodied in critical articles and reviews.

Balboa Press books may be ordered through booksellers or by contacting:

Balboa Press
A Division of Hay House
1663 Liberty Drive
Bloomington, IN 47403
www.balboapress.com
1 (877) 407-4847

Because of the dynamic nature of the Internet, any web addresses or links contained in this book may have changed since publication and may no longer be valid. The views expressed in this work are solely those of the author and do not necessarily reflect the views of the publisher, and the publisher hereby disclaims any responsibility for them.

The author of this book does not dispense medical advice or prescribe the use of any technique as a form of treatment for physical, emotional, or medical problems without the advice of a physician, either directly or indirectly. The intent of the author is only to offer information of a general nature to help you in your quest for emotional and spiritual well-being. In the event you use any of the information in this book for yourself, which is your constitutional right, the author and the publisher assume no responsibility for your actions.

Print information available on the last page.

ISBN: 978-1-5043-6714-1 (sc)
ISBN: 978-1-5043-6716-5 (hc)
ISBN: 978-1-5043-6715-8 (e)

Library of Congress Control Number: 2016916307

Balboa Press rev. date: 10/11/2016

TABLE OF CONTENTS

Author's Note vii
Dedication ix
Foreword xi
Acknowledgment xv
Chapter 1   Pandora's Box 1
Chapter 2   The Realization....................................3
Chapter 3   Thoughts on Writing............................7
Chapter 4   The Piano Bench..................................9
Chapter 5   Hide and Seek....................................12
Chapter 6   Alligators Under the Stairs 18
Chapter 7   The Big Sin..23
Chapter 8   Spinach 30
Chapter 9   No Field Trip for You........................34
Chapter 10   The Palace Theatre 38
Chapter 11   The Grey Suitcases 43
Chapter 12   Don't Look Down the Stairs.............48
Chapter 13   The Card Shop 51
Chapter 14   Come Sit On My Lap........................54
Chapter 15   Katie Joins the Cool Kids 59
Chapter 16   Late for School..................................67
Chapter 17   Layaway...73

Chapter 18	Sleeping with Jesus	78
Chapter 19	Farewell Lancaster Drive	87
Chapter 20	The Voice from the Cellar and the Open Window	92
Chapter 21	The Attic	98
Chapter 22	Little Miss Responsibility	103
Chapter 23	The Girl Scout Uniform	110
Chapter 24	Buon Natale	116
Chapter 25	The Canning Jars	119
Chapter 26	The Allergy Shots	126
Chapter 27	Grant Hill Clinic	132
Chapter 28	The Empty Bra Cup	138
Chapter 29	The Volleyball Net	141
Chapter 30	The White Horse	148
Chapter 31	The Camp Counselor Fiasco	155
Chapter 32	Friendship Betrayed	159
Chapter 33	Blaze	165
Chapter 34	White Trash	174
Chapter 35	David	182
Chapter 36	The Chameleon	193
Chapter 37	The Saint	203
Chapter 38	Safe Harbor	207
Chapter 39	Vertigo	209
Epilogue		215
Afterword		219
About the Author		223

Author's Note

The names and other identifying characteristics of the persons included in this memoir have been changed.

Dedication

This book has been written to encourage the many who have been silenced by fear to reclaim the voice they left behind, to find the courage to speak what's in their hearts; and, finally to be truly heard.

Foreword

When I was a little girl, I always thought my Mom was Stevie Nicks. I knew she wasn't *actually* Stevie, but she contained within her that same ethereal beauty, effortless grace and a certain nurturing, yet mysterious energy that drew me in. I remember her gentle ability to comfort me and the complete feeling of safety I felt in her presence. It was a very good feeling, and I always wanted to be around her. In fact, I still do.

Our bond has only increased over the many years since she tucked me in at night, lulling me to sleep singing "I Will". So heartfelt were the words as she sang that it felt like it was written by her just for me. I would eventually discover it was a Beatles tune. Through the eyes of the grown woman I've become, I can now see her many depths and colors, her passion, her heartache, and her devotion for her family from a new vantage point. This gives me an even greater appreciation for the childhood which she crafted for me, a place where your voice was always heard and no matter what happened, you knew how much you were loved.

The elements that my mother's childhood reflect in this book are opposite to my own. I grew up feeling supported and loved; barely aware of the struggles, financial and otherwise, that went on around me. I remember vacations and holidays, family gatherings and summer fun. There were darker moments of course; and – the occasional cake sent flying across the kitchen due to the actions of irreverent teenagers – but overall the feeling I have looking back is *joy.*

From my own experience of raising a child, I've realized there are no "perfect" parents. However, a wise woman once told me that as long as you always give your best in any given situation, you are on the right track. Now, what your best *actually* is depends on the given day and the circumstances surrounding it, and it is totally acceptable for that *best* to waiver to different degrees. This benchmark is just one of the foundations of my thought process that has been taught to me by my dearest mother. Embracing this idea has carried me through some very difficult times indeed.

Writing this foreword calls to mind of all of the times she has held me up, moments when we laughed or cried together, exchanged a sentimental gift or just spent time together. Slowly, through my adult years, I began to hear more detailed stories of my mom's youth. It's difficult to imagine her as the shy wallflower, not the powerhouse that she is today. Harder to imagine the strength it took her to push through situations that I can barely imagine, in a time unknown to me. But it is her I have to thank for my inability to grasp these concepts, as she imbued me with strength and independence. Certainly, there is much of her in me, both good and bad. I see it in my sense of perfectionism, my work ethic, my devotion to my family, even my style of cooking – where snippets of her influence seep through. There are patterns in my life that emulate hers – the fabric of our lives intimately woven throughout this lifetime. Surely, we see much of each other in ourselves.

Somewhere in my teenage years, a great shift began in her psyche. Although I never knew her to be the way you will witness in these pages, I have seen much growth indeed. We both share the innate desire to grow and change and always be improving upon ourselves. Watching her find her true self, her sense of spirituality, her guidance, and her true love has been miraculous and inspiring; and in fact, infectious. Many ideas and concepts have been opened up to me through her; and, her example has inspired me to reach within myself to find my hidden gifts. There are not many people I know who possess such a vast number of amazing qualities and skills. In her corporate America days, she was a wiz; although never fully experiencing her potential. Graphic design, event planning, interior design, and gardening are among her earthly skills. Discovering the healer within herself, she has given so much to others, both clients and family, through her holistic lifestyle practice – energy work, life coaching, and sharing the vast knowledge of flower essences that she embraces.

Being a part of this book has been a wonderful, eye-opening gift. There have been moments when I just wanted to curl up and cry, unable to believe that someone as sensitive and loving as she could have endured such torment. As she reads me each new chapter, I am transported in time, seeing the places and people she describes as if they are my own memories. I feel blessed to have been brought along on this journey of time travel and to have witnessed the profound healing effects this process has had for her inner child. Few people have the courage to go this deep within, scratching out the demons and facing them head on – only to emerge stronger and more beautiful than ever. There have been many times I wished I could go back in time and sponge up some of the pain, take it upon myself instead and protect her like she has done for me. I could be her sister or her best friend. I could hold her hand and her heart – and in moments of darkness, I would be there to shield her and fill her with love and light. I would sing to her sweetly *"I love you forever and forever, I love you with all my heart..."*

Carrie Fitzpatrick

Acknowledgment

My heart is filled with gratitude for those who have been at my side during the birthing process of this, my first book. The last three years have been a rollercoaster ride during which there were times when I couldn't find the wherewithal to write. The road of life has many detours, yet no matter how many there have been, I've found my way back to these pages. The support of everyone who listened to these stories as they were being written lifted me up with their encouraging words, touting the value the message of this book held for themselves and the difference it would make in the lives of others who will be drawn to read it. I'm also grateful for the confirmation from my clients about the importance of the healing we have done together through my Emotional Archaeology[SM] practice. *Silence* gives voice to the origins of my life's work, the platform for so many to begin to recognize the importance of honoring our emotions.

Along the way, a very special woman has become a treasured friend. Someone I can count on for giving me honest feedback about my writing, someone who has offered continued support in her commitment to make sure I got this book published.

Karen Matheny, you're a gem, your brilliant sparkle and zest for life has kept me going more times than you know.

To those closest to my heart, I know I've thanked you numerous times along the way for your never-ending love throughout this whole process, yet I'm absolutely delighted to share my gratitude publicly within the pages of this book.

To my daughter, Carrie –my muse –you've been by my side through it all, inspiring me to bring my dream of becoming a writer into reality. Thank you for sharing your time and love to support me when I got bogged down, for being my cheerleader when I needed one; and, most of all for always believing I could muster the courage to go into the depths of the dark night within and come out into the light with more strength than I knew I had. *I love you.*

To Kym, my first-born, this has been a long journey and you've been there every step of the way, prodding me along when things became difficult, always believing in me; never failing to get me to dig deeper if necessary. A huge thank you for your tenacity in reading and editing each chapter of this book so fervently. Your incredible commitment to take on the difficult task of reading such intense material, processing it emotionally; then, stepping back to edit it in such a professional manner is more than amazing. And, last but not least, thank you for bringing my vision for the cover to life with your brilliant photography. *I love you.*

Most of all, I offer my loving gratitude to my extraordinary husband, Kurt. You've lived every day, every moment of this book along with me. Always absolutely certain of its value and of my ability to inspire others to find their voices through sharing my experience –you've been my rock. Thank you for your patience, unwavering belief in me, and most of all your unconditional love. *I love you my darling.*

Last but not least to those whom I've loved and lost, I know you've been with me in spirit, I feel your strength and love every day. Thank you for clearing away the obstacles in my path and lighting my way with love.

I know the sound and richness of my own voice because of each of you.

Chapter One

Pandora's Box

I've opened my very own Pandora's Box, simultaneously experiencing its contents through the eyes of a very frightened child and the strong woman I've become.

The process of reclaiming my voice has opened the floodgates of my memory. I find the many heartrending events of my childhood suddenly being recalled in a streaming video, vividly bringing up events long forgotten. Then, there are the dormant ones – things buried in the lost recesses of a frightened child's mind – a mind eager to see the world as a beautiful place despite reality. I am convinced that my own sanity was left intact because of my soul's ability to cloak events with a lack of recall. Children are incredible creatures of light and love, eager to share themselves with others. Oftentimes, it is this vulnerability that acts as a magnet for wounded individuals to act out their hurtful deeds. On the other hand, it is the innocence of their very nature that heals the heart in time.

Pandora's Box

It is from this paradox that I open myself to not only remembering and acknowledging my childhood but sharing it openly with others in the hopes that they, too, will one day be able to connect-the-dots of their childhood and embrace the strengths born from their circumstances. I sit here writing this story – my story – in awe of the soul's ability to shine no matter how tarnished one may believe they've become.

Chapter Two

The Realization

I would like to share something that was initially quite disturbing to me, but later became a blessing in disguise. It was an evening like any other and I fell asleep easily as I settled into bed. The peace was short-lived, as I woke up in the middle of the night suddenly finding myself wide awake from a sound sleep. My first thought was to relax and drift back to slumber, but it was one of those times when I knew that this wasn't going to happen. My mind worked overtime, as I tried to decide if I should get up and go to the bathroom, have some water, make a cup of tea – whatever it was going to take so I could get back to sleep. Instead, I found myself thinking about my grandson and worrying about him. Little things, like him climbing the stairs safely, or making sure his bedroom was childproof since he is just so physically active. I also knew that this wasn't really necessary; he is a very bright child, and his parents have things in place to keep him safe. Try as I might, I couldn't stop playing scenarios in my head. I thought the best thing I could do was to go downstairs to my office and

The Realization

get some flower essences to calm my emotions. I could use the combination of white and red chestnut to help me to turn off the repetitive thoughts and get a handle on the whole over-concern thing. Try as I might, I couldn't seem take any action. Internally, I was asking myself why I didn't go do this because I knew it would work. Instantly, I felt afraid; actually *scared* to get out of bed and go downstairs. In that moment, I was no longer in the present time; as I plummeted into my childhood, I knew what lay behind my fear.

As a child, I used to be afraid of going down the basement stairs because of the dark, but more so because of my brother. My first impulse was to get this thought out of my head and not go there. My brain was not cooperating and neither were my feelings. I had the "I can't move" feeling that I recalled as a child. I could feel myself poised at the top of the staircase getting ready to take that first step down but fearing what might happen next. Even though the light was on there was no assurance it would stay that way. At any given time – generally when I was at least mid-way to almost at the bottom of the stairs, the light would suddenly go off. I'd freeze right where I was, waiting in the darkness and silence anticipating the sound of the voice that would scare the hell out of me.

The words would drift up the stairs, engulfing me. There was a sinister, teasing way that he spoke that made me second guess my every move. I can remember the way my body would tense up until my throat was so tight I couldn't make a sound. I would be petrified and unable to say or do anything but

Silence

listen to the continuous low, droning voice of my brother slowly describing the things that surrounded me in the darkness. He especially liked to remind me of the spiders that he kept in curious-looking jars, never failing to mention how a few had managed to escape, now free to roam. I could feel the taunting behind the voice. One moment it felt as if he were right behind me, and in the next instant, the voice would come from across the room. Suddenly, a flashlight would go on illuminating his face for a brief second or two, then total darkness again. This never failed to send me over the edge into absolute panic, screaming silently. It went on for what seemed like forever until he'd turn the lights back on and act like nothing happened.

Abruptly, I was back in my bed again. I still couldn't shake the feeling of being scared and instinctively reached out for my husband Kurt sleeping next to me. I just wanted to touch him, to feel him there next to me because I knew it would make me feel safe, connected, no longer alone. As soon I touched his arm I felt better, and not so anxious.

After a few minutes, I rolled back over making an effort to convince myself that there was nothing to worry about and that I was safe. Again, the vulnerable feelings of my childhood were taking over. It was in this state of mind that I realized that my brother was there with me in the room, in spirit. Only this time it was very different. Rather than feeling afraid, I felt his presence emanate compassion rather than coldness. I had gotten several "messages" during the previous several days from intuitive friends that he wanted to come "through" to me

The Realization

if I would allow it to happen. I had avoided doing this until I could feel comfortable. I reminded myself that on the polar opposite of my brother's abusive behavior towards me in my youth, there were times when I grew older that we would have deep conversations about the spiritual realm. It was from this place that his spirit communicated with me in the next several moments.

Without words, Junior showed me every instance throughout the years where our relationship permeated my life with fear, all the while undermining my true sense of myself. From this place came the realization that my propensity to worry came from the deep-seated fear implanted within me from growing up with a brother who would always walk on the fringes of sanity throughout his life. A genuine sense of sadness came through him, coupled with remorse for all that he had done to me so mercilessly. I knew he was taking responsibility for his actions and their consequences for the very first time. He had opened the door for me to connect with myself as a little child, allowing me to feel the very essence of the fear that he instilled in me, to see every instance in my life where this fear affected my perception of myself, and how it silenced my voice in so many ways. He gave me the answer to why I had recently been at a standstill in my life, unable to move forward. It was time to reclaim the voice that had been left behind, frozen in fear on the basement stairs. This was his gift to me from the other world, the knowledge that it was time to share my story and to acknowledge the dormant strengths alive within me all along.

Chapter Three

Thoughts on Writing

Writing this story is having a multi-dimensional effect on me. I find myself oftentimes struggling to shed the rose-colored glasses that have shaded many of the stories of my life. While many told from this vantage point still appear to be upsetting and sad, the deeper truth belies feelings more akin to despair. As I sit down and allow myself to go into the void to remember my early life, I am not merely reciting stories. The scared child's fear is mine. The cells in my body reverberate with the conscious expression of each paralyzing moment of silence. I am immobilized at the telling while simultaneously being freed. I find great support from my husband, Kurt, who understands it all without words for explanation. I take care to replenish myself with beautiful music, the lilting vibrations of piano and violin harmonizing my soul once again. I give gratitude for the clarity of each memory, and acknowledge the strength of the child within me as well as the strong woman I've become. In the moment as I write these words, I am enjoying

Thoughts on Writing

the beautiful piece of music streaming through Pandora. Glancing at the soundtrack, I find its title is "Heart of a Child." Once again, the adage "there are no coincidences" finds me.

Chapter Four

The Piano Bench

Kindergarten is my first memory of being singled out, not by other children, but by the one person who was supposed to lead by example, my teacher, Mrs. Desmond. On a day that started out like all others, it was the time of day when she would read to us. I remember taking my place on the floor, tucking my dress neatly under me as I carefully sat down on the small pillow made of a knobby feeling fabric the color of a robin's egg. As I crossed my legs, I gently smoothed out my dress covering my legs "just like a little lady," the way our teacher had instructed. There was a buzz of excitement all around me as the rest of the kids took their places in the circle, anxious to hear the day's story. We always had story time gathered in front of the straight-backed wooden piano in the corner of our classroom near the bright sunny window that overlooked the playground.

Once everyone was gathered, Mrs. Desmond joined us, ceremoniously walking through the space she had taught us

The Piano Bench

to leave in the circle for her to do so. Tucking her long yellow flowered dress beneath her, she sat down on the piano bench and settled in. I waited anxiously for her to tell us the name of today's book. As she turned the book over, I caught sight of *The Gingerbread Man*. My favorite! I was instantly bouncing in my seat waiting for her to begin. Mrs. Desmond looked my way and I remembered how she liked us to sit still. I tried my best. As the story unfolded, my excitement overtook me and I started talking aloud about what was going to happen next. I loved this story! In my reverie I must not have heard her tell me to be quiet. Suddenly, in the midst of reading, her pleasant story voice suddenly disappeared. Then, she just stopped reading. In the blink of an eye, she was off her seat and coming towards me. All fell silent. In one fell swoop, she pulled me out of the circle – my skinny frame offering no resistance as she grabbed my arm. Across the floor I sailed, my body sliding on the linoleum, heading towards the piano. I saw the other kids pull back, their eyes wide with fear. Before I knew what was happening, she began to push me under the piano bench. My head hit the underside while at the same time my bony knee banged into the wooden frame, sending a jolt of pain mixed with fear through my tiny body. I was shaking like a leaf and began to cry.

Leaning down towards me her eyes wild, she pointed her finger in my face and told me not to make another sound. I felt her sit sat back down on the bench. I swallowed hard and brought my hand to my mouth to stifle any sound. I laid there shivering with fear as I stared at the back of her legs. Try as I might, I couldn't

Silence

stop the hot tears from rolling down my face, puddling on the floor under my cheek as I stayed in place, curled up in a little ball. I'll never forget the sight of the seams in her hosiery nor the back of her black pumps. Her feet were so close that the smell of shoe polish filled my nose. I held myself as still as a stone for fear that any movement might cause me to bump into her legs. My eyes were riveted on the faces of the children that I could still see. They looked blank and fixed with fear, surely a reflection of my own. Not a sound escaped from anyone. Mrs. Desmond continued with the story, right where she left off without skipping a beat.

After the first few words, the only thing I heard was my own heartbeat pounding in my ears. In what was by any definition cruel, Mrs. Desmond made me stay under the bench, even after story time had ended. I lost track of time praying for her to let me come out again. My body felt stiff and sore but I still wouldn't budge an inch for fear of what wrath might come my way next. Finally, I saw her black pumps making their way across the floor towards my tiny prison. In a harsh voice that I didn't recognize, she told me to come out. I carefully unfolded myself as I slid out from under the bench, my beautiful dress crumpled. Dutifully, I smoothed it back down as best I could and limped over to my seat. I sat there as quiet as a mouse. Somehow even at this young age, I knew that "little Debbie" wasn't in the room any longer. I had gone somewhere deep inside where it didn't hurt anymore. As I grew older, I would perfect this ability. It became my salvation.

Mrs. Desmond never taught our class again.

Chapter Five

Hide and Seek

There's a very good reason why cellars in old houses tend to bring out the primordial fear within us. Besides the obvious feeling of being underground, cut off from any easy escape, we have an inherent fear of the dark. Or should I say, "the things that like to live in dark places." Cellars exist in perpetual darkness until, thanks to Mr. Edison's invention, they are transformed by light. Still, just before the light bulb goes on, our minds have time to think about what may be lurking down there. Feeling rather comforted by the glow of light, we take those first few steps downward, all the while trying to ignore the lingering thought about what may exist in the recesses of those places where the shadows live.

My brother knew how to use this fear. He was even more talented at creating it. This was especially true when it came to me, his kid sister, seven years younger than he was. I was the perfect quarry for Junior's ploys – easy pickings some might call it. He had an uncanny ability to sweet-talk me into doing

Silence

his bidding. He would give you a look that emanated a calm innocence that was utterly unnerving. He could make you doubt any misgivings you had about him, no matter what may have transpired previously. So flawless was his performance that you would be swept away, becoming part of the play, cast as exactly the character he had in mind for you.

Things would start off innocently enough, just your average game of hide and seek. One of us counting to one hundred, while the other one found the perfect place to secret themselves away. The basement always provided the best location for hiding places with neglected stacks of boxes, garments hanging on metal racks, and the day's laundry neatly pinned to the rope clothesline stretching from one side of the room to the other. An array of odds n' ends stuffed under the stairs could readily be arranged to conceal oneself amidst the shadows. The only illumination available at the flick of a switch was the light bulb at the bottom of the stairs. In the deeper recesses of the cellar, bare 60-watt bulbs waited patiently in their plain white sockets for someone to reach up and pull the chain that would bring them to life. Like most children, I found hide and seek to be fun, resourcefully finding places to "disappear" until one's whereabouts were uncovered; howling with laughter when found out. So it was, one Saturday afternoon while my mother was away at the grocery store, that my brother and I set about to play the game. There were two important rules; the first being no peeking; the second, all the lights stayed on. Several rounds were played out; each of us taking a turn

Hide and Seek

trying to find the other. On my next chance to hide, I spied the "perfect" spot. In the far corner of the basement was a sturdy wooden work bench with a space below. It looked safe enough, no cobwebs in sight. There was even an old torn blanket thrown across it that I could use for cover. I squatted down and duck-walked my skinny frame under the fabric. I gave the corner an extra tug to make sure I was completely hidden. The fabric got stuck on something for a moment. No matter, I was tucked away out of sight. As the count reached one hundred, all went quiet. Knees scrunched up to my chest, I sat waiting still as a mouse, certain it would take a while to be found. Then out of the stillness, came the unexpected yet distinct sound of a "click." I could have sworn it was the switch by the stairs, but it couldn't be. Lights on was the rule. I kept silent, not wanting to give away my hiding place. Several seconds later, the faint snap of a pull chain resounded, then another. The basement was plunged into absolute darkness. "Junior, turn the lights back on!" I shrieked. No response. "It's the rule, it's the rule," I pleaded. There was no reply. I was frozen in time, my mind racing, trying to understand what was happening. Then, out of the blackness came a sound like fingernails on a blackboard, followed by a chilling whisper slowly uttering six words, "Ready or not, here I come."

My seven-year-old mind couldn't fathom what was happening or why. I was petrified of the dark, and it was obvious, "the rule" no longer applied. Somehow, it felt instinctively better to keep silent and unseen. Ears perked up anticipating the

Silence

next sound, I waited, breathing as quietly as I could. Finally, it came. The sound of someone walking with a limp, the footfall followed by a heavy dragging that sent chills up my spine. An almost inaudible whisper moaning my name oh, so slowly, over and over again. I was quaking inside and out, terror mounting in my body. "Where, oh where are you?" Sinister yet calm, the voice sing-song as it penetrated the darkness. Waiting, I couldn't move. More shuffling around in the dark. A box being pushed on the floor, the cardboard scratching against the cement. "Come out, come out wherever you are," came the invitation, taunting me to be brave enough to face my tormentor. Time stood still. Cat and mouse unmoving; waiting for the next move to be played. A faint click, the smallest ray of light danced eerily on the concrete; the rules were changing. I valiantly nudged my head close to the edge of the blanket, trying to catch a glimpse of my brother without being seen. The light bounced around the room, as he searched for his prey. "I wonder where you are," came the taunting statement. "I hope you didn't decide to hide under the workbench. You wouldn't want to disturb those jars I left under the blanket." My mind immediately connected the dots; he didn't have to spell it out. "The Bug" collected spiders, amongst other ghastly things, and most of all, he knew I dreaded encountering arachnids. "All it would take is a nudge to set them free, I may have used the blanket as cover," Junior. called out. My heartbeat pounded in my ears as my mind raced back to the moment when I adjusted the blanket earlier. Had I dislodged the covering? The room plunged back into darkness. It was no longer just my menacing brother in the game; he had brought company. At this very moment, there could be one of those hairy long-legged horrors making its way up my back, unseen. Every molecule in my body urged me to bolt from under the bench, yet I sat transfixed by the unknown, barely breathing. There was no real escape.

The sound of footfalls on the stairs broke the silence. One...two...three...four...they kept their solitary pace until the twelfth stair was reached. I heard the distinct turn of the metal doorknob and the wail of the door opening on its hinges. Unceremoniously, the door closed, the latch sounding its pronounced click as it did so. "Was it really over?" "What if he comes back?" my left-brain pondered, while all sorts of scenarios played themselves out. So deeply embedded was the threat that I was pinioned into place. Minutes ticked away, feeling like hours. Logic took hold. He had to be gone. It was physically difficult to move. My legs had gone numb from being scrunched up, immobile, for so long. Wiggling side to side, momentum moved my frozen limbs as I freed myself from my prison. I stood, trepidation surrounding me, as I got my bearings in the gloom. My hands worked feverishly brushing over my body in the hopes of dislodging any unwanted companions from my clothing. I let my eyes get acclimated to the darkness. As vague outlines began to come alive, I plotted my course towards the stairs. Taking baby steps, from stiffness as well as terror, I moved closer and closer to the stairwell. Hesitantly, I reached out for the light switch, feeling my way along the wall. Click! The room erupted with brightness. Shadows fled,

Silence

replaced by familiar shapes of pajamas and underwear drying on the indoor clothesline. Reluctantly, unsure of what lie ahead, I reached out for the banister and made my way up the cellar stairs. Hand contacting the knob, I turned it gently and pushed the door wide open. Everything was quiet. I rounded the corner from the kitchen to the dining room. There sat my brother, plate of fresh baked chocolate chip cookies and milk in front of him. Turning towards me with a smile befitting an angel, crumbs on the corner of his lips, he said, "Wasn't that fun?"

Chapter Six

Alligators Under the Stairs

Learning to become mobile is one of the biggest challenges we face as children. Navigating stairs heads the top of the list. As a child, it's an incredible physical experiment, yet the thought of climbing somehow enthralls us. Compelled by the exciting promise of seeing what our world looks like from "up there," we are innately willing to conquer great heights to find out what lies at the top. Much to the chagrin of our parents, we seem to be almost magnetically drawn to stairs as little kids. They employ safety gates to hold us at bay for as long as possible. Succumbing to the inevitable, our parents teach us how to mobilize ourselves for climbing by using both our hands and feet, keeping our center of gravity low enough to maintain balance during the ascent. We learn that our buttocks are the safest way to come down stairs, sitting on one step after another until we reach terra firma once again. So it goes, until we learn to use the handrail, gaining our balance and traversing stairs with ease.

Silence

When we reach the senior years of our lives, stairs may once again become a physical challenge, this time much more formidable, since we are no longer mesmerized by what lies at the top. We are just happy to think we can get there without too much difficulty. The contest to get our weary bones up an entire flight can be insurmountable to some. Indeed, we may find ourselves using the same methods we did as children to conquer the imposing trek upwards.

Unlike most children, stairs – especially steep ones – ranked high on my list of things I'd prefer to avoid. Being afraid of heights compounded things. Unfortunately, when I was growing up, along with our bedrooms, the one and only bathroom resided on the second floor of our home. I dreaded the several daily non-negotiable trips that had to be made to relieve my apparently small bladder. A formal "announcement" that I was going upstairs always preceded my journey. I guess it was some sort of safety net in my child's mind, guaranteeing that someone knew my whereabouts, just in case something untoward happened. Holding onto the handrail, my fingers wrapped around the wood snugly, I'd begin my climb. Eyes looking downward, I'd watch each foot raise and lower, sliding my hand up the rail slowly, never losing contact with the wood. With each movement, I knew I was getting closer to the top, counting the number of steps – fourteen to be precise – made me focus on the task at hand. Once at the top, the real challenge began. Trying with all my might, I fought against the feeling of being pulled backwards by some unseen gravitational force,

Alligators Under the Stairs

and reluctantly let go of the handrail. Taking a deep breath, I edged myself across the foyer. Reaching the wall, I found safety at last.

This was all a piece of cake compared with going down. There was the real challenge. Poised on the landing, I reached out to make contact with the banister. My fingers wrapped around it, clutching it for dear life. Half-heartedly, I made my first move, once again wrestling with the peculiar magnetic pull downwards. "Slow and steady, slow and steady," I repeated to myself as I held my breath and headed for the bottom, struggling to keep my balance.

As most trips were without incident, I began to slowly gain confidence. That is, until the day my brother Junior intervened. That fateful evening, I was using the bathroom. Finished, I came out onto the landing. The stairwell ahead was bathed in a combination of shadows and soft white light from the ceiling fixture. Taking a deep breath, I gave myself my traditional little pep talk before going down, reassuring myself that it wasn't really all that steep after all. Bracing myself with the handrail, my slippered foot dropped over the edge, and plunked down on the stair below. "One," I counted under my breath, "two, three, four." I was on my way and feeling pretty good about my progress. As I raised my foot for number five, my concentration was broken by the startling words echoing up the stairwell; "Don't forget what's under the stairs."

Silence

 I froze, instantly falling prey to my fourteen-year-old brother's frequent dire warnings about what lived under the stairs. There were "things" waiting patiently for just the right moment when the stair would mysteriously open, causing the unsuspecting; namely, me, to fall helplessly into the hole below. Junior had told me stories about how kids had small pet alligators that their parents would throw down sewers as they grew too big for their cages. He made a point to mention that they could find their way into the strangest places once they were on the loose. "Crocks," as he would call them, could grab and swallow a child before anything could stop them. Every detail of the gory event was doled out, slowly, in that special creepy voice that he always saved for this kind of thing. The thought of their giant gaping mouths, sharp white teeth covered with bright red blood held me prisoner on step number five. My reverie was silenced by his taunting voice, floating eerily up the staircase, "You never know which step it's going to be." The chilling words hung in the air as my technicolor imagination recreated the horrid scene that might await me. Suddenly, his face peered around the living room wall. Looking up at me with squinty eyes, his bared teeth clicked together, creating the perfect theatrical prop that sent me over the edge. "Momma! Momma!" I screamed at the top of my lungs. My brother's face disappeared instantly, replaced within moments by my mother's as she searched for the cause of the commotion. "There's alligators under the stairs!" I cried, as I shook from head to toe, still clutching the railing with all my might. She looked me square in the eyes in that way that mothers have,

Alligators Under the Stairs

her eyes searching to connect with me in that place past fear. Repeatedly assuring me that there was nothing to be afraid of, her soothing words finally reached the recesses of my mind. The fear began to melt, as she coaxed me down, one step after another. By the time I made it to the bottom, my brother had conveniently disappeared. My mother and I sat down together; I was safe and sound. As I nestled in on the couch, covered by a warm blanket, my mother returned to the kitchen to finish making supper. Feeling better, I let myself relax as I snuggled up with a big pillow. The room was quiet, except for the drone of the television set. As I began to drift off, the eerie voice came from behind the sofa whispering the warning, "Just wait, they'll get you next time."

Chapter Seven

The Big Sin

Being a storyteller, I love photographs. Looking at pictures gives us a glimpse into the life of a person – it freeze-frames forever a moment in time. I can spend hours looking at old photographs, recalling memories or wondering about the people in them; perhaps creating stories about what was happening at the time the picture was taken. I connect with another time and place as my imagination animates them in my mind, igniting emotion. A relative recently gave me an old picture he had found of me, taken when I was the tender age of seven. I looked like a vision of innocence in white, dressed for my Holy Communion; my tiny hands poised in prayer – rosary beads draped over them. Kneeling down, my body was posed to turn towards the camera. My golden curls peered out from underneath the veil I wore, the cherub-like face beaming as the shutter of the photographer's camera clicked, suspending time forever on film. As I gazed into my own eyes, I wondered how many people had looked at me, thinking how angelic I looked and how happy I must have been at my Holy Communion. They

The Big Sin

could never in their wildest dreams imagine what happened that fateful day from looking at this photo, as it was actually taken before the "big sin" took place.

The year was 1960; and, like all good seven-year-old Catholics, I was all ears when our teacher, Sister Mary Gertrude, supplied us with the crucial information we needed to know before we could receive Holy Communion. I still remember the way her chin moved ever so slightly as she spoke, held in place by the stiff white apparatus that held her face prisoner, covering all but her eyebrows, eyes, nose and mouth. I often wondered if it hurt her to speak from inside the awful contraption, the archaic habit worn by nuns of her order. But speak she did, and we dared not miss a word, or we would suffer the consequences of a wooden ruler coming down across our hands. I, like the others, was rapt with attention. She drilled us on the procedure to be followed at our First Confession. To attain absolution, we had to inform the priest of our sins; including any impure thoughts we may have had that could have led to wrongdoing. Above all else, we must be truly sorry for committing these acts; repentance was essential. I had always been a pretty docile kid, so when it came to breaking the Ten Commandments, I was pretty sure I was in the clear. Still, I lost sleep worrying about some potentially forgotten sin; hearing Sister Mary Gertrude's voice warning us about the horrors of committing sacrilege should we receive Holy Communion in an impure state of mortal sin.

Silence

Finally, the time came for my First Confession. Kneeling in the pew, wringing my hands and shaking the entire time, I awaited my turn. I watched, eyes wide open, as one-after-the-other my fellow sinners, their faces pale with fear, disappeared into the dreaded confessional box. There was no way of knowing what the ordeal was like by catching a glimpse of their faces; each one exited with their head bowed low and hands in prayer, just as we were taught. My observation ended as Sister Mary Gertrude pointed her long wrinkled index finger at me, her black habit making her look something akin to the grim reaper. This was her signal for me to stand up from the kneeler, turn towards the waiting box, and walk with my hands folded in prayer towards my salvation. Reaching the confessional, I pulled back the heavy dark red velvet curtain. With knees knocking and hands shaking, I stepped into the void. I knelt down facing the small closed window, holding my breath and waiting in silence. With a ceremonious creak, the screen slid open revealing Father Giussani's visage behind it. Instantly, in practiced response, the words, "Bless me Father for I have sinned," squeaked out of my parched throat. I still hadn't recalled any real "sins," so I made a few up to make sure I hadn't forgotten some horrid misbehavior. *It never dawned on me that doing this was a sin in and of itself.* Once satisfied that I was truly sorry for my misdeeds, the priest assigned my penance – two Hail Mary's and one Our Father. In response, I recited the sixty-seven words of The Act of Contrition – verbatim, having rehearsed it over and over again. Father Giussani spoke the Latin words that absolved me of my transgressions. Following

The Big Sin

the identical route the others had taken to the altar, I knelt down and humbly recited the prayers I had been given as penance. Now I would be considered pure enough to receive communion.

The next morning would be the consummation of the ritual for which we had been so carefully prepared. Heartened that I was still in a state of grace, having been obediently cautious enough not to commit any sins prior to going to bed, I slumbered. My dreams were peppered with uneasy scenarios of tomorrow. When I awoke in the morning, there was no rattling of pans nor scent of eggs and bacon drifting in from our kitchen. No, indeed, this morning I was not allowed to eat or drink anything, lest I pollute my body prior to receiving the Body and Blood of Christ. My mother, by no means a devout Catholic herself, was tempted to give her little girl some breakfast just the same – perhaps at least some toast and tea. Indoctrinated by Sister Mary Gertrude, there was no way I'd take the chance and risk it, despite my mother's assurances that neither God nor his Son would mind the transgression.

When we arrived at St. Jerome's, the flock of white-clad girls was easy to spot; and, after kissing my mother, I reluctantly took my place amongst them. It was easy to blend in as I joined them, the crinolines under our dresses creating an exaggerated shape that made us look like a field of mushrooms. The commanding voice of Sister Mary Gertrude pulled me out of my daydream. The cluster of white quickly dispersed, lining up to fill the pews – their straight wooden backs creating order from chaos as we filled row after row. The church fell

Silence

silent. Everyone stood up in unison as the priest and his minions, the altar boys, appeared. Father Giussani spoke to the congregation, his well-chosen words filled with fire and brimstone, emphasizing the seriousness of the rite of passage unfolding before us. His stern gaze focused momentarily on each one of us. As he caught my eye, a wave of fear and nausea swept over me. It was just the beginning of what was about to transpire. I sat immobile, eyes transfixed on the altar as the mass unfolded. Suddenly, the sound of a single clap pierced the air. Hearing this signal, every one of use rose simultaneously from our seats; Sister Mary Gertrude had taught us well. Hands clasped in prayer, tips of our fingers touching the bottom of our chins, we took turns exiting the pews – one girl from the left – one boy from the right – and walked in practiced gait to our awaiting destiny. My turn came…eight slow, deliberate steps and I reached Father Giussani. Up close the golden chalice looked foreboding, as the priest reached in and withdrew the round wafer from within it. The Body of Christ, held firmly between the priest's index finger and thumb, came towards me as I closed my eyes, opened my mouth, and stuck out my tongue to receive it. As I turned away and began making my way back to my seat, my very own personal Hell began.

I tried to swallow rather than chew the Host, as we had been taught. Since I had nothing to eat or drink for hours, the wet wafer plastered itself onto the dry roof of my mouth. I began to panic. My mind was certain of one thing, I had to make it back to my seat before anyone noticed what was happening. Knowing

The Big Sin

every eye in the congregation was on me, I forced myself to walk reverently back to my seat without giving my secret away. As I slid into position on the waiting bench, I was beginning to choke, my throat convulsing. I forced myself to keep silent. Kneeling down, hands folded in prayer, I used them as a cover so that no one would notice what was happening. Sister Mary Gertrude would be livid if she caught sight of me making a scene. I frantically made attempt after attempt to dislodge the wafer with my tongue, but I couldn't muster up enough saliva for it to budge. My eyes filled up with tears and threatened to roll down my cheeks. *I prayed for it to dissolve, but it wouldn't.* Another minute and things would be obvious to everyone. I couldn't contain things any longer. In desperation, I slid my index finger into my mouth slowly and deliberately so as not to draw attention. My fingernail connected with the sticky mass, as I excavated it from its captivity. Thank God this made my mouth water a bit, so I swallowed hard and got down as much as I could. Carefully, I removed my finger and brought it back to its place in prayer position. Then, I saw the telltale wafer. I dared not try the same maneuver again. In a decision made from the confusion and fear of a young child, I rolled the evidence in between my two fingers; keeping it hostage until I sat back on my seat. I was petrified. Sliding my hand slowly under the edge of the pew, I slid it off onto the wood. For a moment, my ordeal was over. Then, the realization of my actions hit like a ton of bricks – I had done the unforgivable! I touched the sacred Body of Christ; only the priest was allowed to do this! Worst of all, I had disposed of the remaining fragment like a mouthful of

Silence

unwanted lima beans secretly wiped off under the kitchen table. Sister Mary Gertrude might not have seen what I'd done, but God certainly did. *It was over for me; no priest could assign a penance big enough for Him to forgive me.* Tears rolled down my face silently, my mind echoing the inevitable edict. I had committed "The Big Sin." *Forget Heaven, I was going to hell.*

Chapter Eight

Spinach

What do you say to your father when he's reminiscing about when you were very young and you can't connect with the story? When you have no recall, but the look on his face is searching for recognition, eyes imploring you to validate what is being shared? The consummate non-answer – a smile and a quick hug – became my modus operandi.

I grew up with my father existing mainly on the periphery of my life. At times he felt more like a phantom than real to me. We would connect momentarily, then he was gone. An hour here or there, with a trip to Morton's Dairy usually being the highlight of our time together. I remember standing in front of the massive wooden counter waiting patiently for the double scoop pistachio cone with chocolate shots to be handed first to my dad, then to me. My eager hands would gratefully accept the offering, the wafer cone wrapped neatly with a napkin. He'd order black raspberry and join me at a table either inside or outside depending on the weather. I imagine we made small

Silence

talk though I don't recall. I was just a little kid on a limited timeline focusing mainly on not letting my ice cream drip. The few stories I remembered were the ones he probably chose to forget. Being much younger than the rest of my siblings, I was saved from the escapades of my father's addiction to alcohol in his younger years. However, I did not escape unscathed.

One afternoon my mother sent me on an errand to buy a large can of spinach at the nearby grocery store. It was a brisk ten-minute walk just outside of the boundaries of the project where we lived. Shortly before dinnertime, money in my pocket, I headed off alone promising to be right back. Finding the item on the shelf, I headed to the cash register, paid, and took my bag with a thank you. Dusk began to settle in as I returned, so I sped up a bit and was halfway home when I tripped on a pothole in the asphalt that was unexpectedly deeper than it looked. My foot twisted painfully as I lost my balance.

The sequence that followed was simultaneously both blindingly fast and sickeningly slow. The paper bag slipped out of my hands and into the air. Somehow both the sack and my face landed in exactly the same spot at precisely the same time, the rim of the can hitting the bone directly over my left eye. As I got to my feet it took a moment for the pain to register, as I was preoccupied with a deep scrape on my knee. Everything slammed into my consciousness at once, as I felt the warm liquid stream over my eye and down my face. *Blood! Blood! I can't see!* My mind and my voice screamed in unison. In an effort to stop the bleeding, I grabbed the bag from the ground,

Spinach

tore off a piece and plastered it over the cut, then walked as fast as I could to get to my house. Someone's mom heard me crying and came running to my aid. Suddenly, there was my mother running towards us from the other direction; one of my friends had heard the commotion and ran to get her. Once in our kitchen, she remained calm as she took the soggy pseudo bandage off my face. Quickly realizing that my eye was intact, she placed a heavy washcloth packed with ice over the cut to slow the bleeding and cleaned the blood off my face to minimize my shock. A neighbor drove us to the emergency room while my mother gently reassured me that I was going to be fine. My ill-fated collision with the spinach can resulted in several stitches to close the wound. Later than night, carrots replaced the leafy green vegetable originally slated for dinner.

I dreaded knowing that I had to return to the doctor to have the stitches removed. I ticked off one day after another on the calendar heading toward the fateful day. It never came. Instead, my father decided that it was a simple task to remove them himself. He convinced me that it wouldn't hurt a bit as he lured me towards the bright light of the dining room window so he could see better. Holding myself as still as I could, I sat in front of him as he pulled a pair of nail clippers out of his pocket. Second thoughts overcame me and I started to whimper. He told me to close my eyes, saying it would be over in a minute. All he had to do was snip the knot on the end and give it a little pull. I squeezed them shut as tightly as I could and waited. As he laid his fingers against my brow, I felt the cool stainless steel

Silence

of the cutters as they began their work. *Dad was wrong. It did hurt. Something had gone awry.* Deep inside I knew I was right. Unceremoniously, he finished a few minutes later. Content with his work, he grabbed a beer and headed to the sofa where he fell asleep.

I made the mistake of looking in the bathroom mirror. To my horror, the removal procedure had left the area over my left eye puffy and crimson red, stiff little sutures sticking out here and there amidst the hairs of my eyebrow. Anxiously, I waited for my mother to return home. As soon as I heard the creak of the door, I started to cry. Greeting her with an angry, swollen eyebrow, it took her only an instant to guess what had transpired as she glanced towards my sleeping father, telltale clippers on the end table next to him. Ignoring her husband completely, mom set to work making things right with an ice pack and a pair of tweezers. Muttering under her breath in Italian, no doubt so I wouldn't understand her, she gently removed the remaining fragments of my father's handiwork. Rewarded for my bravery with cookies and milk, I curled up on a chair in the living room.

Naïveté being my best friend, I didn't realize that my father had been drinking when he attempted the "simple" feat of removing my stitches – my mother, however, knew better. It never occurred to me when she kept her calm that her silence was merely a reflection of the process of burying yet another episode starring her inebriated husband. In my mother's mind, it was more *water under the bridge* – a tacit river of misdeeds that would one day reach flood stage drowning my father within it.

Chapter Nine

No Field Trip for You

Looking out the schoolroom window, I see my fellow third-grade classmates standing in front of the bright yellow bus, their faces filled with gleeful anticipation. The sound of their voices, while indistinguishable, lilt through the air towards me. Guessing at words I could only imagine, my mind painted a picture of their thoughts. As I sat silently watching from a distance, the long line dwindled quickly as one after the other, they eagerly got on board. Today's field trip to the aquarium had been the subject of endless banter for the last several weeks in our classroom, so much so that I had memorized the entire schedule of events for the day. Daydreaming, I envisioned sharks, their silvery gray bodies languidly moving through their habitat, mesmerizing all who watched from the other side of the glass. Floating before me were images of large tanks with beautiful colored fish in all shapes and sizes creating an underwater panorama. I imagined the water show with dolphins leaping and playing, their vocals emanating through the air with glee. This and more lay before

Silence

the kids on the bus. Their day would unfold one magical moment after another.

The school bus pulled away from the scene, taking my daydreams along with it. Before me now was an imposing blackboard and a teacher I vaguely knew. My day was destined to tick by one long minute after another sitting in a foreign classroom with kids I'd seen on the playground but didn't really know. They all had an advantage over me in that respect, each of them knew an intimate detail about me something I could not hide or deny. I was the poor kid who couldn't go on the field trip because we couldn't afford it. Left behind, pure and simple, because of lack of money.

Sure enough, I had been escorted into their room by my teacher as everyone settled into their seats. I stood head down by her side as she hurriedly explained the situation to her associate. The conversation shared between the two educators was overheard by the kids in the front row and quickly spread throughout the room like wildfire. Their teacher pointed to a leftover desk in the middle of the room and directed me to take a seat. All eyes were on me as I did so; some reflecting pity, others contempt for the intrusion into their space by an outsider. A few boys snickered and made wisecracks under their breath, designed to mortify the skinny girl with the pigtails. I sat down in the midst of them, cemented into my chair like a statue. Silently, I was praying that somehow they would just ignore me, yet instinctively knowing I was just too easy a mark for the bullies in the class to bypass.

No Field Trip for You

The day began in earnest. My thoughts drifted in and out; sometimes I'd hear what the teacher was saying, and other times I'd zone out completely. Thirty kids all around me, yet I was so alone. I didn't belong. Although not an altogether unfamiliar feeling, it was made worse as I thought about the empty seat on the bus that could have been mine. The sound of my name being called pierced the fringe of my consciousness. Apparently, gauging by the laughter in the room, Mrs. Owen had been repeatedly attempting to get my attention. My embarrassment was clearly emblazoned across my face, the scarlet heat rising uncontrolled to its surface. On high alert now, I tried my best to focus attention on the lesson being presented. I obediently turned the page of my textbook to the day's assignment and got busy.

Before I knew it, lunchtime was upon us. This was going to be bad. I just knew it, as the cafeteria was the perfect ground to strike. I found a seat at a table as quickly as I could and hoped for the best. There should have been at least one loner in the class that would seek me out, someone to commiserate with for at least a few minutes in this endless day. A short boy with rumpled hair, glasses and an unevenly buttoned shirt made his way over to my table. He sat, one empty chair between us, mouthing a quiet "hi" before opening his lunch bag to quietly consume its contents. A peanut butter and jelly sandwich sat on wax paper in front of me. My mother had cut it in fours as she always did; the familiarity somehow felt comforting in the midst of everything. My first bite coincided with a direct hit

Silence

to my face by a spitball launched with precision and followed by laughter. I ignored it as best I could, focusing instead on the clump of bread that stuck to the roof of my mouth. One bite after another, I made it through pretending not to notice. All the while I felt myself shrinking little by little, praying I would just disappear silently, leaving not a trace of the day's ordeal, my sandwich, or myself behind.

The rest of the day wore on until the sound of the school bell tolled its end. The classroom emptied quickly as I sat in my chair slowing putting away my papers and books, a delay constructed to avoid everyone. Giving them more than ample time to clear the school yard, I walked out of the room that had been my solitary cell for the day having done my time.

I'll never forget the irony of dinner that night. We had fish sticks.

Chapter Ten

The Palace Theatre

I've always been fascinated with movies; the love of cinema was engrained in me at an early age. I would look forward to the special Sundays when my mother said we could go to a picture show. Together we'd wait anxiously at the bus stop across from the Cities Service gas station in anticipation of the ride downtown. Our destination was the Palace Theatre for the double-header: two movies played back-to-back concurrently all afternoon long for one admission price. Hard to imagine a deal like that these days, but it was the norm back then.

Mom and I had a special ritual for this event. The bus would let us off in front of Lifshutz, our local five and dime store. There, we would get a bag of fresh popped corn with real butter on it. The red and white striped bag was longer than my arm and cost a dime. Then, it was down the street to the confectionery shop where we would each get a quarter pound of our favorite candies. Mom always got nonpareils, the dark

Silence

chocolate discs covered with tiny white crunchy pellets. I opted for the Boston baked beans, which were actually peanuts with a hard brownish-red coating that would dye your fingers if you weren't careful. I remember watching the woman behind the counter putting the small white paper bag on one side of the machine, and on the other, the counterweight. She'd carefully fill the waiting sack, sometimes giving me a conspiratorial wink as she added a few extras, tipping the scale in my favor. I'd give her the quarter I'd been clutching in my hand, taking the bags in return. With a smile and thank you, we'd head out the door. Hand in hand, we would head for the theatre, only a short distance away. One last act completed the ritual. My mother would slip the popcorn bag under her coat and the candy into her big pocketbook, as a knowing look passed between us. The concession stand inside was too expensive for our budget so we'd "sneak" our goodies inside. We weren't the only folks privy to this ruse, as we'd inevitably bump into someone in the theater who had just stood in line ahead of us at the candy store. A quick "wink" between adults acknowledged their shared conspiracy.

What a thrill it was to approach the huge marquee, lights blazing even in the middle of the day, enticing passersby to come in. The giant black script letters proudly announced the landmark: Palace Theatre. As she led the way to the ticket booth, I'd follow my mother up to the window watching her ceremoniously slip the fifty cents through the small opening. In exchange, the woman behind the glass would slide two

The Palace Theatre

admission tickets through the slot. Before walking through the grand entrance, there was always the obligatory look at the posters announcing the features we had come to see.

Once inside, we would always sit in the same place. We'd head to the seats located adjacent to the exit door on the right side of the theatre. This guaranteed a wide swath between rows, a necessity to allow my mother to sit comfortably given her girth. Placing her purse under her seat, she would fold her coat neatly in thirds placing it over the back of the chair; I'd obligingly sit next to her, mimicking the rite. Soon, the lights would dim, signaling everyone the show was about to begin. I always loved the way the massive burgundy velvet curtains covering the stage would part ever so slowly, exposing the movie screen as if it were a well-kept secret. I could feel the anticipation build all around us as the lights went down and the previews started. We all waited eagerly to see what the future held in store for coming events. The chatter of voices ceased as the feature presentation began. You could hear a pin drop as the opening sequence of the movie began.

Intermission always provided the chance to walk around, use the restroom, or visit the concession stand, if you were inclined to do so. My mother would always nudge me shortly before the movie's ending so we could use the bathroom before there was a line. We'd watch the last scene over our shoulders as we headed up the carpeted runway, stopping short of the door to savor the final moments. The powder room at the Palace was majestic. One wall held massive gilded mirrors hung from

Silence

the ceiling, coming to rest on an elaborate granite ledge large enough to hold baskets of fresh flowers. There were Victorian style sofas covered in rich dark red velvet scattered throughout the room. Women strolled up to the mirrors, fussing with their hair or putting on fresh lipstick. I sat admiring them as I waited for my mother to emerge from the bordering restroom. If I wasn't too preoccupied, I'd catch my mother putting a few coins into the attendant's hand, thanking her for the disposal towel. She always saved a little something for this purpose, no matter how much we scrimped elsewhere. On our way back to our seats, we would stop at the water fountain to quench our thirst.

The entire opening scenario was repeated as the house lights dimmed and the curtains parted once again for the start of the second feature. As we nestled in, an older man slipped into the seat next to my mother. He politely tipped his hat to her before removing it and placing it on his lap. I could see my mother's discomfort with his presence – the telltale raising of her right eyebrow signaled her distaste. She clearly preferred an empty seat to the stranger's presence, especially when other spots were clearly available. As the film started, we both began to relax, indulging ourselves in the entertainment, until I was distracted by an ever so slight movement of my mother's hand. I watched out of the corner of my eye as she slowly raised it to the side of her head, adjusting the small skullcap she wore. As her hand returned to her lap with the same precision, I caught the glint of the long silver hat pin. My eyes followed its trail, as it expertly hit its mark – the stranger's hand resting on my

The Palace Theatre

mother's thigh. Silencing his response rather than risk further embarrassment, the "gentleman" promptly rose, turned, and fled down the aisle towards the exit. The trademark "eyebrow" raised once again accompanied by a look of sheer satisfaction.

The empty seat remained.

Chapter Eleven

The Grey Suitcases

My father's younger years were pretty much unknown to me. I'm certain that the dad my older siblings knew was not the same guy that I did. Growing up, it was easy enough to fill in the basics by piecing together tidbits I would hear during adult conversations. Evidently, word had it that after Vic came home from a stint with the Seabees, a branch of the Navy, he took to drinking and womanizing. Over time, it seemed my mother and he had come to an *understanding*. Apparently, one day he overstepped his bounds. He left when I was around eight years old. My mother never said a bad word about my dad to me. Sometimes I would feel awkward spending time with him. This had more to do with lack of familiarity than dislike. By the time my father and I began to develop a real relationship, he was around fifty-eight years old; I was twenty-two. My mother would oftentimes comment that at this age, he was finally becoming the man she thought she married, although she wasn't forthcoming with any details. One of my earliest memories of my father is the day he left us.

The Grey Suitcases

One morning, mom said we were making a special trip downtown. She was looking for some fabric to make curtains for one of the neighbors, so we would be heading to Grant's department store on Main Street, her favorite place to get material. I loved going through the bolts of fabric they had, imagining what she could sew next. Mom would always let me choose some five and ten cent remnants from the markdown bin, destined for some creative project – what could be better? Although I didn't know it at the time, my mother and I had actually set out on a fact-finding mission.

Riding the bus towards our destination, I was surprised when my mother reached up and pulled the cord above the window signaling the bus driver that we wanted to get off at the next stop. Normally, we'd get dropped off in front of Grant's. I looked at her, puzzled by her actions. Without my needing to ask any questions, she quickly told me that everything was fine, we were just going somewhere else first. I followed her wordlessly down the aisle and got off the bus, feeling like a grand adventure had just begun. Once on the street, we walked a short distance, coming to a stop in front of three identical apartment buildings, their immense towers of discolored golden bricks looming skyward. My mother was unusually quiet and obviously contemplating which one to approach. Would it be building number one, two or three? *Hmmm, what was she looking for?* I thought to myself. Choosing the one in the middle, I counted the cement steps – one through eight, as we made our way to the landing.

Silence

It was quiet as we entered the small empty foyer, the only sound the creak of the door announcing our arrival. Just inside, a tall yellowed wall covered with embedded mailboxes caught my mother's interest. Having never been inside an apartment building before, I was mesmerized by the rows of small plastic windows, each shielding a square of paper marked with an apartment number on top, and just below these, the occupant's name. Without a word, my mother ran her finger down each row, slowly searching for the missing element of our clandestine operation. As she did so, I stood off to the side, absorbed by the mystery unfolding before me. I was caught off guard when her finger stopped abruptly about midway down the second row. *Something felt very wrong.* Mom didn't budge, index finger locked in place, her body unmoving. One long sigh emanated from her, filling the space with a palpable heaviness as she turned away. Heading towards the door, I fell into step behind her, but not before gazing at the place her finger had occupied. Apartment fifteen's occupant shared our unusual last name. I was baffled. *What was the importance of what we just found? Did it herald a long lost relative, perhaps? Why then, did we turn away?* No information was forthcoming from my mother. Instinctively, I knew not to ask any questions.

Outside in the fresh air, the color came back to my mother's face. In the stillness, we stood together for a brief moment before my mother took my hand and said, "Are you ready for some shopping?" Our earlier encounter dissipated like smoke

The Grey Suitcases

on a windy day. Just like that, off we went heading towards Grant's as if we had just stepped off the bus.

Despite the pretense of a sunny disposition, my mother wasn't herself as we perused bolt after bolt of fabric. What would normally be fun and exciting felt like more of a chore as she finally settled on a printed cotton for the kitchen curtains she planned to sew. On our way up to the main level of the store, it was obvious that something besides the climb of the twenty or so stairs was weighing heavily on my mother. I focused on the treat that I knew would greet us when we reached the landing. Displays of every kind of cookie imaginable lined the wall, their glass covers waiting to be slid open by the saleslady. She'd reach in with a piece of waxed paper and remove two large Hawaiian lei cookies and put them into the white paper bag; one for each of us. I was certain this would cheer my mother up, as we both adored the taste of the combination of shortbread, chocolate and coconut which had become our ritual for the bus ride home. A ten cent investment guaranteed to put a smile on your face.

My mother's unnerving quiet returned, permeating the time we spent getting back to the projects. I made my cookie last as long as possible, savoring each bite as if it were my salvation – a way to keep the absence of conversation at bay. Home at last, Mom suggested I go outside and play until she called me for dinner. I felt somehow like I was abandoning her to the unknown, but did as she asked. A few kids were out back, so I joined in until suppertime arrived and they answered the call to

Silence

come and eat. Figuring it was only a matter of moments until I heard my mother's voice echoing the sentiment, I headed home. There was no familiar rattle of pans, no smell of food cooking, and no sign of my mother at the stove as I opened the door to the kitchen. Instead, I heard voices coming from the living room – my mother and father were engaged in conversation. *It wasn't loud. It wasn't an argument. It wasn't right. It felt all wrong.* As I peered out from the kitchen, my eyes caught sight of the two big grey suitcases that sat ominously, one alongside one another, stationed by the front door. "You can take your bags to your apartment, you don't live here anymore," were the last words I heard my mother speak, as their somber conversation came to a dead halt. An eerie silence filled the air as my father's hands reached down to meet the heavy leather handles. Fingers sliding slowly around the grips, he lifted them off the floor and walked like a ghost out of my life.

Chapter Twelve

Don't Look Down the Stairs

Sometimes memories are shrouded behind thin veils, offering just enough cover to keep a portion of them hidden. The soft wind of remembrance blows through your mind, revealing more than perhaps you really want to see. Doubt replaces clarity, or maybe it is just a protection mechanism of the mind. Too much information. Too much fear. Little children should have nice memories, not frightful ones. The wound, too unbearable, is covered with the gauze of amnesia. One day, when we are ready, we remember.

There were two twin brothers in our neighborhood that were like night and day. They neither looked alike nor had the same temperament. My brother Junior sometimes hung out with one of them, Larry, although most people tended to steer clear of him. Try as I might, I cannot connect the dots of exactly why I went over to their house that day, except I know I was looking for my brother. It was Larry who answered the door when I knocked and asked him if Junior was with him.

Silence

"Yeah, c'mon in, he's down the cellar," he said, shrugging his shoulders nonchalantly. "Just tell him to come home okay?" "Tell him yourself, kid," came the sarcastic reply, as he pushed open the door and moved aside. I wavered for just a split second; he started to close the door. I went in. That was mistake number one.

I went down cellar – *mistake number two* – although it would take me a few minutes to realize it. Preoccupied with calling to my brother as I went down the stairwell, I didn't immediately hear Larry behind me. No reply was forthcoming. "He's in the back room, he can't hear you," came his ominous explanation. I kept going, but only momentarily. There was no light emanating from further in the cellar. *My brother couldn't be there.* The realization hit just as Larry snickered. The sinister sound echoed in the quiet of the catacomb that surrounded us. I never realized just how creepy he was until I turned around and looked up into Larry's dark eyes. "My brother's not here, you're lying!" came my words, slipping out with false courage. He was blocking my way out. Bravado was never my strong suit. I froze. I felt like a mouse being watched by a cat, trying to find a way past without being caught. A noise that sounded like it came from upstairs suddenly broke the silence. It was just enough of a distraction for me to escape. I was almost to the top of the stairs before I realized there was no one following me. A distant voice was speaking words that sounded garbled at first, then came the recognition that it was Larry. I realized that he was directing these comments towards me, saying,

Don't Look Down the Stairs

"What's the matter, I wasn't going to do anything...really, I was only kidding...just turn around for a minute and listen to me, c'mon." He suckered me in, my naiveté being my downfall. I looked over my shoulder. Larry was standing at the bottom of the stairs, pants down, his hands on his privates. A look of sheer satisfaction was on his face; his wicked Cheshire cat grin lasting only briefly before he began to laugh.

Scrambling towards the door, I nearly bumped into my brother. No words needed to be exchanged, the look on my face said it all. Junior headed towards the basement, warning me not to follow. Larry's voice pleaded. This time I didn't look down the stairs.

Chapter Thirteen

The Card Shop

There's an old adage that goes, "save the best for last." In this case, it's more like the worst, at least for me. There is a huge feeling of vulnerability in writing this chapter that exceeds the others. I want to wrap my inner child in a big blanket, snuggle her close, and say this stuff can be left out of the book. In fact, I've echoed that sentiment a few times along the way while writing, and each and every time the result is the same. Reaching into myself, I look into my own eyes as a child seeing the innocence return bit by bit as each chapter evolves. I know that including this segment is as essential as breathing.

The first begins rather unpretentiously, as I recall how much my mother loved sending cards. No event was ignored that contained the possibility to become a Hallmark occasion. Budget-wise, buying cards was what she would consider a *splurge,* but worth the investment. A trip to the card shop on Main Street would always last at least an hour as she poured over the racks, looking for the perfect sentiment for the person

The Card Shop

she had in mind. Finding it equally enjoyable, I'd peruse them right along with her, always ready to put my two cents in about which card I liked the best. The man that owned the shop frequently puttered about the aisles, straightening cards and making chitchat with the clientele. There were always people going in and out, although most of them picked out their card, wrapping paper, or ribbon quickly and were on their way. He didn't seem to mind one bit that my mother took her time; she was a *regular* after all. Because of this shared familiarity of the card shop, my mother was comfortable enough to leave me alone there one afternoon at my request. I wanted to purchase a Mother's Day card for her *all on my own*. It was a big moment for me! My mother was going to go to the little shop next door to have a coffee. She promised to be sitting right in the window where I could see her as soon as I came out of the card shop. The owner overheard our conversation and nodded while throwing a wink my mother's way, signaling he'd keep an eye out for me.

I immediately set out for the section with the Mother's Day cards lined up row after row. There were so many to choose from. *How would I ever pick just one?* After a few moments I was engrossed in my search, trying to find the perfect card for my mom. The sentiment had to be just right; it had to be *special.* I was so immersed in reading the cards that I didn't notice the owner move in alongside of me. Startled, I moved back a bit as he came closer. "Thought you could use a little help there," he crooned, while surreptitiously slipping behind me. "I'm doing okay, thank you," I said meekly, already uncomfortable. Before

Silence

I knew it, he had one arm straight out over my shoulder leaning against the rack, and the other over my right arm. The feeling of him leaning into my back was scaring me, although at the tender age of eight, I had no idea of why. *It just felt very, very wrong.* He leaned farther forward, pressing into my back as he picked a card off the rack with his large hairy hand. The strong smell of his body odor invaded the space as queasiness hit my stomach like a ton of bricks. Then I felt him begin to rock himself against me, something hard hitting my backside as he did. *Why was he doing this to me?* I tried to wriggle free but couldn't move. He was muttering something incoherent to me. "I found a card, I like this one," I uttered in an effort to get him to stop. He didn't seem to hear me. I swallowed hard, holding back the feeling of wanting to vomit right on the spot. Panicked, I summoned courage I didn't know I had, and stomped on his foot as hard as I could, maneuvering away before he knew what was happening. Dropping the card as I ran down the aisle towards the door, I made the mistake of looking back as I got to the door. There he stood in front of the Mother's Day display, zipping up his pants.

When my mother saw my face that day and listened to what I told her, she had held me and told me everything would be okay. We never went to his store again, nor did my mother ever speak of the incident afterward. Several months later, as we walked down Main Street together, I spied a giant *Going out of Business* sign on his storefront. My mother's trademark uplifted eyebrow said it all – *what goes around comes around.* Now there's a sentiment you'll never find in a Hallmark card.

Chapter Fourteen

Come Sit On My Lap

The innocence of a child is a precious commodity, one that merits respect and deserves to be cherished. It is the light we all seek; some to bask within it, others to own it. The hungry ones feed off of it, gorging themselves until they feel satiated, leaving tattered fragments behind. Being young and tender, children don't even realize the loss until they grow older, and many not even then. The return to innocence is a long road. Remembering the faces of those who stole from us a piece of our childhood can cause anguish. It also holds the key to who we have become and why. The gift of knowledge and awareness when you are old enough and strong enough to use it is indeed powerful.

Looking back now from the vantage point of having written almost this entire book, I feel stronger in the core of my being. Owning the words I put on paper and truly listening to myself in the process has opened my eyes to so much. I share this

Silence

particular story knowing that by telling it, I reclaim still another piece of me.

After the dissolution of my friendship with Katie, I felt very alone. Abandoned. Somehow from that place of loneliness, I made a connection again. There was a girl named Belinda that I did not really know. She lived out of our immediate circle in the projects, out on the periphery of our comfort zone as it were. My mother took odd sewing jobs here and there, and had been sought out by a Mrs. Broderick to make a slipcover for a chair. I accompanied her to the Broderick home on her visit to take a look at the furniture that needed covering. Belinda and I bonded that very first meeting. We recognized each other's reticence and were drawn to each other because of it. She was a year older than me; her sister two years younger. Their entire family had immigrated to the United States when Belinda was school age.

I would accompany my mother during fittings as she worked on the sewing project, getting to know Belinda better. Our relationship grew to a comfortable enough place that I would occasionally go over her house without my mother. Although I was welcome to visit, Belinda was not allowed to visit other people's homes – an edict decreed by her father. I remember the way their family interacted with one another because it was very different from mine, especially when their father was present. He was the irrefutable head of their household; Belinda's mother was at his beck and call. A friendly woman otherwise, she would become quiet as a church mouse, literally

Come Sit On My Lap

walking around with her head down in his presence. This was strange behavior in my eyes, since I was raised predominantly by my mother who deferred to no one.

Mr. Broderick was a big man; not overweight, but *built like an ox,* as some would say. He wore his hair slicked back and always had a scruffy looking face. Brown curly hair would pop out from the collar of his t-shirt and covered his arms and hands, making him look like he was wearing a sweater. His hands were immense with rough cut fingernails that always looked grimy.

Belinda's dad wasn't what I would call mean; he didn't speak in a tone that was gruff, but you instinctively knew that his word was law. His mere presence conveyed the message of his sovereignty. His daughters became more reserved in his company; there was almost an edginess to their behavior. Whenever I was visiting, as the clock in their living room chimed four o'clock, I knew it was time to head home; that was the rule. Mr. Broderick came in from work on weekdays shortly afterward, and Belinda would need to *attend to her father,* as she would say. I wasn't exactly sure what that meant, but knew that playtime was basically over.

Weekends were different. Momma Broderick would always be busy in the kitchen, the smell of cabbage and potatoes permeating the house as soon as I walked in the door. Belinda's father always seemed like he was in a better mood on Saturdays, sitting comfortably in his enormous brown chair in front of the

Silence

television set with Anna, his youngest daughter on his lap. She would generally sit there most of the time as Belinda and I would quietly play a board game at the kitchen table. Then it would be Belinda's turn. Her father would call her name and she'd take her sister's place while I waited at the table. I never understood the ritual, but assumed it was just what fathers liked to do. So the day that Mr. Broderick asked me if I wanted to sit on his lap along with Belinda, I didn't hesitate – it made me feel special.

Belinda and I sat across from each other, one knee for me and one for her. I felt the warmth of his leg almost instantly; it was if he were on fire. He bounced both of us up and down for a minute with a broad smile on his face. The grin should have made me feel more at ease, but being unused to the attention of a father, it felt odd. I looked across at Belinda to find that she didn't look all that happy, but I figured this was just an everyday thing to her anyway. Without a word, Mrs. Broderick came in and put a small glass dish with some pickles on the end table next to her husband and left just as uneventfully. Distracted momentarily by her presence, I was drawn back to the moment as I felt the large hand slip under my bottom and squeeze, the fingers pushing in between my legs. I seized up in fear. *What was he doing? It wasn't right – it didn't feel good. Daddies didn't do this; did they?* I looked at Belinda imploringly. She stared back blankly, her face as emotionless as a doll, the skirt of her dress rumpled where her father's other hand was partly visible.

Come Sit On My Lap

Tears flooded my eyes in an instant as I sat trapped, staring at my friend. "Mrs. Broderick, Mrs. Broderick," I whimpered, breaking the frozen silence. I turned my head towards the kitchen and repeated the plea a bit louder this time, in case she had not heard me. Although I was looking directly at her, tears rolling down my face, she turned away.

"Go away, you cry baby," came the gruff words whispered in my ear as Belinda's father gave me a shove off his lap. I moved to the door with the speed of a gazelle. Drawn momentarily to look back towards my friend Belinda, she held her index finger in front of her pursed lips, cautioning me not to tell anyone, her eyes pleading with mine for my silence. Grasping the doorknob, I turned and fled. Belinda and I never spoke again.

Chapter Fifteen

Katie Joins the Cool Kids

Growing up in the 50's and early 60's was such a different life than nowadays. The pace was definitely different, as we grew up without the technology of today. Never mind there was no Internet, there were no computers! We talked to each other on party lines, if you had a telephone. No one I remembered was lucky or wealthy enough to have a private line. Anyway, talking on the phone was usually reserved for adults, not kids. Mostly, we talked to each other in person. If you wanted to know if someone was home, you'd walk to their house to find out. As kids, we developed our own way of inquiring. We'd basically "sing" the name of the kid we were looking for at least three times in succession while standing on their back porch. If they could come out to play, they'd answer the door. You never did this at supper time, and everyone respected this rule. While it sounds complicated, it worked just fine – we kids had quite a network of communication.

Katie Joins the Cool Kids

I lived on Lancaster Drive as a kid. The address sounds posh – like it should be on the rich side of town. It wasn't. Instead, it was part of a housing project. We moved there when I was five and ready for kindergarten. In its heyday, it was a pretty good place to live overall. There were different sections to the project; we lived close to the entrance of the property off of the main road. There was a total of thirty-two duplex apartments arranged in long rectangle. Each building had a shared covered porch, the wooden front doors painted white. The back entrances faced the interior of the block, and consisted of an individual small concrete porch with three steps and a railing where metal milk boxes awaiting their once-a-week delivery competed for space along with kids' muddy shoes. The giant backyard created community space akin to a very long football field, intersected with sidewalks lined up like grids between the brick two-story buildings. Every family had a clothesline directly outside their back door. Clothespin bags hung on the poles. If you wanted something creative, you'd visit my mother and put in your order for a handmade one that stood out on wash day. She would turn your favorite fabric into a one-of-a-kind design; thereby earning a few dollars for herself while making the neighborhood women happy. These little touches were the hallmark of our enclave of homes that identified our section of the project. My mother somehow set the standard for Lancaster Drive. She'd keep the small plot of grass out front under control employing an ancient push mower, bushes trimmed neatly with a hand clipper. A border of zinnias, grown from seed packets bought at the five-and-dime

Silence

store, brightened things up, and seedlings were shared with neighbors who didn't have a green thumb. Mom's favorites were the long-stemmed gladiolas she loved. In her own way, my mother helped people create something beautiful from a lackluster postage stamp of a yard. In turn, it transformed our block into a place that felt like home. My mother acted in the capacity as "official" caretaker, being known to pick up any stray pieces of paper or the like that might be found along her walk around the block each day. She set an example that most people followed, including the kids.

Everyone pretty much got along with one another. While some families were known to keep to themselves, others were friendlier. There were about a half-dozen kids my age that hung around together. We would play hide and go seek around the neighborhood just before dark, or build tents on the clotheslines out of old sheets and blankets when it wasn't laundry day. There was a playground across the street that had a paved basketball court that the boys loved, while the girls tended to group together on the swings. On summer weekends, sometimes parents would put together dances for the kids, hooking up a record player and a few speakers in the pavilion. Everyone pitched in whatever records they had, while someone's teenage brother acted as deejay. Somebody's mom would make Kool-Aid, and others baked cookies. The girls danced together, while most of the boys hung out around the periphery. At least they showed up, though probably more for the eats than anything else.

Katie Joins the Cool Kids

It was here in the midst of simpler times, that I made my first best friend. Her name was Katie. She lived two doors down from us with her mom, dad, three brothers and sister. Her parents spoke with an accent which I loved. I found myself emulating the way they spoke whenever I spent time there. Her father, a rather large man, had a way of nodding his head in my direction and smiling as I tried my best to sound like one of them. There was always a frenzy of activity happening at Katie's – that's life when you have a large family. As I recall, her brothers were spoiled rotten, able to sit around while Katie handled most of the chores. I'd help her out sometimes so she could get outdoors to play. Strangely enough, cleaning house was A-Okay as long we were spending time together. Our friendship grew with the benign loyalty that comes from being there for someone when they need you.

I recall many Saturday mornings having breakfast around their huge table. It was akin to having a meal with the Walton family of television fame. Her father would sit on one end of the wooden mammoth and her mother on the other; when she actually sat down, that is. Katie's mom spent most of her time running from kitchen to dining room. Huge clear glass bowls filled with chunks of white bread were placed next to a similar sized vats of pure maple syrup. I remember how everyone would pierce a piece of doughy Wonder Bread with their forks, then plunge it into the glistening pool of dark syrup. The trick was in the "spin" on the way out of the bowl. The technique allowed them to get the morsel into their mouths

Silence

without so much as a drip hitting the table cloth. The kids had all mastered it from endless breakfasts before. Never quite getting the right combination of speed and twirl necessary to keep from making a mess, I employed my own method of placing my hand under my fork to catch the inevitable dribble. While we ate, Katie's mom was back in the kitchen whipping up the next course. Through the tiny doorway she'd appear, juggling a heaping skillet full of scrambled eggs with green peppers, her potholders protecting her hands from the heat. As soon as the pan touched the tabletop, each person took their share. Once on their plates, the familiar ritual would begin as everyone began to squish the yellow and green concoction with the tines of their forks until the pieces became tiny morsels. It was here that I learned the habit that stays with me to this day. I always mash my scrambled eggs. I must say there is something delicious about the taste that doesn't seem to translate into larger chunks. Perhaps it is the sweet childhood memory that enhances each mouthful.

Remembering what it was like sitting around their family dining table, the child within me recalls the hunger of wanting to be a part of something larger than myself. My siblings were all much older than me; early childhood memories of time spent together are few and far between. While my mother and I were always close, Katie's family still drew me in. There's something about a big family that creates a giant bubble of life. When things are good, everyone floats along together, while turbulent times jeopardize the fragility of the invisible sphere,

Katie Joins the Cool Kids

stretching it to the point where its demise appears imminent. Yet, things always seemed to bounce back again. There was a comfort in feeling that interaction. Within these surroundings, Katie and I grew up together from kindergarten to fifth grade. She became more like a sister to me with each passing year.

Growing up without the benefit of "extra funds," we used our imaginations instead of our pocketbooks to devise all sorts of games we could play together, from the simple to the elaborate. Summer vacation from school created the time for our creativity to soar with games that would carry on over a succession of days. We'd set up elaborate tent "houses" on the backyard clotheslines. Katie and Barry were one family, Ann and Matt, another, while I opted for the rather elusive David, who had stolen my heart at the tender age of five over a pretend cup of tea. The boys would ride off on their tricycles to "work", the location relegated to someone's front porch. Meanwhile, the girls stayed home with the children, our favorite dolls playing their parts. From the vantage point of age, I'm certain the boys agreed to play because there was delicious food involved. Our mothers donated peanut butter and jelly sandwiches, as no one was yet allergic to peanut butter, fresh-baked cookies, and apples to serve as "groceries" that we'd offer up to our pretend family. Then, there would be the special treat we all waited for on a hot day. As my mother came out the back door of our house, all ears would perk up at the sound of the familiar crack of the handle on the metal ice cube tray, signaling the release of the frozen Kool-Aid cubes from their icy enclave. She'd wrap

Silence

each one in a white paper napkin and hand them out one by one to each waiting kid. A sweet treat guaranteed to bring a smile to one and all.

Time passed, and the lemonade stands and tent houses became a thing of the past. School took over our days, making weekends suddenly become special. Our horizon was expanding past our immediate neighborhood. Elementary school housed kids from all over, not just our project. There were those whose families owned their own houses with fenced-in yards and cars in their driveways. These children took vacations past their own backyard, and had ice cream sundaes from Morton's Dairy whenever they wanted to. This was our first foray into the recognition of having less than others. Before then, we were pretty much all in the same boat, unaware of any different lifestyle but ours.

Nonetheless, Katie and I walked to school together with the rest of the gang virtually every day. We all stayed pretty close as kindergarten turned to first, second and third grade. Playing house gave way to reading books, taking walks around the block, and figuring out arithmetic problems together, weaving the fabric of friendship as we grew up together. "Puppy love" bloomed like wild flowers strewn along the playground fence. Emulating our play families, Barry was the apple of Katie's eye, while I continued to be spellbound by David. Back then, boyfriends were more like buddies – we were young and smitten. Sleepovers at Katie's became the backdrop for quiet whispers about cute Barry was or how blonde David's hair

Katie Joins the Cool Kids

was in the sunlight. Secrets shared after the lights went out and flashlights came on under the covers cemented our best friend status.

Our friendship felt good, changing but somehow solid. That is, until fourth grade. In that fateful ninth year of my existence, the first brick was laid in what would become my life as a wallflower. To be perfectly honest, I never saw it coming. I was always the timid, quiet one of the group. Katie had always been more outgoing, which was great, until it led her out of the confines of our tight-knit friendship and into the realm of the "other" kids. Studying at the school library together got replaced with her going over someone else's house after school. I was not invited. Hanging out together would get interrupted by a telephone call, quick excuses, and a change of plans. Knocking on her door on weekends would elicit a brother who would answer, tell me she was busy or not home, and close the door in one fell swoop. Suddenly, gone were the two of us sharing secrets. Other girls with more exciting stories to share, new and different things to do replaced the mundane and familiar. I had nothing new to offer. We still walked to school together, but she'd leave me flat as soon as we arrived. I didn't fit in with the new crowd. I never would. Katie had joined the cool kids.

Alone on the school grounds, bewilderment became my new friend.

Chapter Sixteen

Late for School

Walking to elementary school alone, I would oftentimes talk to myself for company. I'm not quite sure if this is just a natural inclination for people born under the sign of Gemini, although I know it certainly seems likely, after all – we do have a twin in there somewhere. Anyway, I became company for myself, as my best friend, Katie, had more or less disappeared from my life early in fourth grade. It was a lonely time. Even if I was walking with some of the other kids, I suddenly seemed to be on the outskirts of it all, as if everything had become dismantled without her at the helm.

The customary route that we took to school involved crossing the playground and climbing up a small hill, then meandering through the other sections of the projects, diligently looking both ways before traversing any streets we came across. Since we did not use the city sidewalks, there were no crossing guards ensuring our safety. After walking at a good pace for about fifteen minutes, you'd reach Jimmy Simpson's house,

Late for School

which meant you were almost there. Once you rounded the bend, the "big hill" would come into view. It loomed before us, a challenge to be met boldly. On a good day, the hill was somewhat difficult, but we'd hold hands as we climbed. Nearing the approach, we would always get a running start, propelling ourselves upward. If someone, more than likely me, was having a tougher time, a bit of support made things manageable. The school sat on a clearing at the top of the peak, a jewel crowning our Mount Everest.

There was another route to school, but no one ever went that way from our neighborhood. While it had paved sidewalks most of the way, it entirely circumvented the project where we lived. It entailed walking "the long way;" basically going around everything that comprised the projects and took more than twice as long. There were no shortcuts to be taken.

One especially wintry day, I was jolted awake by the sound of my mother's voice, urgently calling me out of the abyss of dream time. Our alarm had not gone off – and it was a weekday! Although it had snowed during the night, school was still in session. Back then, it wasn't canceled at the sign of the first snowflake or hint of a storm. Heck no! You had to wake up with a Nor'easter blowing heavily in progress before that happened. In an effort to waylay the damage of being late, I dressed in a hurry. My mother insisted on a nice, hot oatmeal breakfast – you never ran out the door without food in your belly under any circumstances. I put on my coat, scarf, boots and the apparatus necessary to face a New England winter.

Silence

Meanwhile, my mother put her handwritten note spelling out the reason for my tardiness into a small envelope, expertly licking the edge and sealing the contents inside in a single movement. She deftly slid it into the zippered front pouch of my book bag for safekeeping. This parental document was integral at Thomas Jefferson. No one dared show up at school late without this prerequisite, which you were to instructed to take directly to the office upon your arrival.

As I walked out the door, alone and late, I considered taking the alternate route to avoid navigating the big hill. Nothing mortified me more than being tardy. It had happened only once before. The whole scenario was playing out in my head ceaselessly; walking to the office, meekly checking in, answering questions about why I was late. Next, sitting in a line-up while the secretary reviewed my note, looking back and forth from its contents to my face, as if pondering whether it was a forgery or not. The worst of it was being escorted to your classroom, where the teacher would glare at you and the kids snickered. That was a scene to be avoided like the plague. Flashback to reality, there was a decision to be made now. I was already late, but I didn't want to be seriously late. So, with shaky determination as my guide, I took the familiar, shorter route. Things went relatively well as I neared the first climb, but halfway up I lost my footing and began to slide backwards. Bracing myself by leaning forward, I pressed my hands into the snow to gain my balance. My fingers clawed at the snow from inside my red mittens as I inched my way upwards, afraid to

Late for School

stand up lest I take another tumble. Reaching the top, I stayed on my knees until I maneuvered onto some flat space, made by the footfalls of the kids earlier this morning.

The rest of the walk was much easier, so I made up for lost time. Within sight of Jimmy's house, I knew I was nearing the challenge that lie ahead. I began giving myself a pep talk, speaking out loud since there wasn't anyone around. Rounding the bend, I stopped in my tracks. What loomed before me was more akin to a snow covered mountain than a big hill. I immediately wished I had taken the other way, but here I was. It looked perilous at best, and I wasn't exactly the mountain climbing type. My mind flashed a warning: *Turn around now – go home while there's still time. Don't be such a chicken,* taunted a voice, reminding me of earlier times when kids made fun of me. *I can do this,* I told myself, assured for the moment that there was at least no one watching. The tracks left by the others would mercifully offer me a path to follow. There was no other choice, I thought; just put one foot in front of the other and don't look up, and keep your eyes riveted on your feet and the next foothold. Up I went, slowly at first. In an effort to feel more confident, I reminded myself that it wasn't that bad – that I was doing okay. While I didn't have anyone's hand to hold, they had left their mark to follow just the same.

Lost in the reverie of the moment, I lifted my foot up to reach the next imprint. A sudden twist of my ankle confirmed I had missed the target. Losing my balance, I fell on my side and began to slide downwards, the snow having been made slippery

Silence

by an overcoat of freezing drizzle that had begun earlier. *I had to stop...fast!* Valiantly, I dug my boot heel into the crusty snow, effectively halting my descent. I caught my breath. I had lost about half my ground, but that wasn't the worst of it. The fall caused me to veer significantly away from the path, leaving me, quite literally, on a slippery slope indeed. Tears began to well up in my eyes. I was scared and shivering. Stranded, I knew the only way to keep going was to try and get back to the trail. Slowly, I inched my way back by sitting on my butt, crunching the snow with my feet as I kicked my heels into it to gain some traction. As I got closer, I reached for the salvation of the indentations in the snow. By some miracle I managed to flip myself over without falling. Staying bent over, for fear of another tumble, I thrust my fisted mittens into each hole ahead of me, one after the other until finally, breathless, I reached the summit. Crawling on my hands and knees, I made doubly sure I was far enough from the perilous edge to stand up. *Hallelujah! I made it! I stood up.*

Alas, the feeling of euphoria was short-lived. Looking down at myself, I was a mess. My pants were embedded with wet snow, my hair sweaty and hanging out of my hat. The only good news appeared to be that I was alone; there were no gawking onlookers to contend with this morning. Mittens caked with snow, I brushed myself off, little good that it did; the ordeal had taken hold of me. The only thing keeping me from crying was knowing my face would probably be chapped for days from the cold, leaving a tell-tale sign of this whole mishap

Late for School

that would cause even further embarrassment. *Go home, go home, don't go inside* – the message flashed through my brain, begging to be considered. There was no easy way to accomplish such a feat, as the obvious choice was to slide back down Mount Everest. Taking the long way home would risk being seen from a classroom and was out of the question. These two options were implausible at best, so off I went to the office to undergo the process for being late.

Arriving in my classroom more than one hour past the expected time, another inquisition began. A concerned Mrs. Jennings asked way too many intimate questions in front of my classmates about my current disheveled condition. Everyone was watching and listening. The investigation over, head down, I took my seat. With icy stares keeping me company, I sat all day in those wet pants, feeling stupid and ashamed. My mind heard unsaid jokes about the skinny little Debbie; words their looks shouted at me. At some point in the day my clothes dried, but the feeling of a cold chill stayed with me inside and out, never leaving. I always felt like I was on the periphery of the class from then on, but I was never late to school again.

Some feelings linger forever, showing up in unexplained peculiarities. Simply put, even now I cannot abide being in wet clothes for very long, even a swimsuit. The recollection of this old memory and acknowledging the intensity of the feelings within it has given me the reason behind my idiosyncrasy. The awareness of this elusive truth touches the fabric of my very being, drying the tears of my youth.

Chapter Seventeen

Layaway

What a wonder it was as a kid to ogle the gigantic windows of Lerner's Department Store, the colorful displays filling me with awe. I could walk around and around the huge centerpiece of the storefront, its unique shape surrounding me on all sides with mannequins wearing the latest styles as they beckoned you into their world inside the glass. My footsteps would echo on the marble tile floor as I made endless circles admiring the clothes, imagining what I might look like in them. I loved the creative displays with their magical lighting making everything look picture perfect, as if it were all there waiting for you and only you.

This was my pastime while my mother and I waited for the bus downtown. Out front, she'd keep watch for its arrival, allowing me this adventure, although I'd always land up pulling her into my fantasy by insisting she come see an outfit that enthralled me!

Layaway

Sometimes, we'd actually go inside the store to look around. Pulling open the big glass doors with a whoosh, we'd be drawn into the magical expanse before us. Carpeted floors created a dramatic hush as I took it all in, deciding what to look at first. I spied something that caught my eye in the window, eagerly pointing it out to my mom while pulling on her sleeve for added emphasis. Getting to look at it up close was a thrill. Gingerly touching the fabric of the woolen red coat with the black buttons and soft faux fur collar, I felt like I was in heaven! My mom took a closer look, checking out the way it was made; then, ran her hand down the sleeve, seeking the price tag that dangled below. She flipped it over and studied it momentarily. I waited with baited breath for her verdict. *Could we possibly afford this beauty? Would I be able to try it on?* As her gaze shifted from the tag, Mom's face said it all without a word. A sigh escaped me in response. For a split second, everything was quiet between us. "Let's keep looking around, there's so much to see," she said, taking my hand. Abandoning the red coat on its hanger, we headed to the back of the store where the closeout items hung forlorn waiting to be rescued. I feigned interest as my mom flipped through the rack, my heart already stolen.

It was getting late and time to take our place outside so we wouldn't miss our ride home – the last bus of the day. On our way out, we slowed down a bit as we approached the red beauty patiently waiting just for me. My mother bent down and whispered, "You could sure use a new coat, maybe next time we're here it will be on sale." Beaming with the possibility, I

Silence

daydreamed all the way home about wearing that beautiful coat, feeling the soft black fur around my neck keeping me warm, and prayed they'd mark it down soon.

Time went by with days turning into months, the red coat slowly taking its place amidst archived memories begotten by wishful thinking. Announcing a visit to my grandmother's house one day, my mom said we could look around downtown before walking the remainder of the way to her house. "Yes, we can go by Lerner's," came my mother's answer, a reply to my yet unspoken question. Excited by the anticipation of seeing my coat again, I flew past the mannequins in the storefront, uninterested in their garb. I had one destination in mind as we entered the store, heading towards the location like someone lured in by a homing beacon. *Wait. It's not here.* I had memorized exactly where it had hung. *This had to be the place.* My eyes scanned the store, looking for something red, while my mother asked the saleslady for some assistance. "Oh, yes, I remember that coat. You should have gotten it earlier, it's all sold out," she stated bluntly, as her words trailed out into the ether, taking my dream with it. I felt crushed, as if someone had knocked the wind out of me. *It just couldn't be true.* "Hey, Debs, come on. Maybe we can find you something else that you like," offered my mother, in an attempt to cheer me up.

Off we headed towards the familiar back wall, although I suggested that we might as well leave. In my mind, there was no replacement worthy of buying, even if it was on sale. I stared at my feet rather than look at any of the other beautiful clothes we

Layaway

were passing by. Then I felt a nudge, my mother's elbow gently breaking the spell of disillusionment that held me prisoner.

I looked up at my mother's face. She was grinning from ear to ear as she pointed directly ahead of her. There it was, the red sleeve sandwiched in between the other markdowns. I ran over to it, pushing the other items away to expose its full majesty. *My red coat! The last one!* I closed my eyes for a second and caught my breath. My mother reached out and turned over the price tag, the moment of truth having arrived. *Fifty-percent off!* "Can I try it on, please…please?" I inquired, more a statement than a question as off the hanger it came, into my outstretched arms. In our excitement, we hadn't checked the size. My hands virtually disappeared beneath the sleeves as I tried it on, the shoulders slouching a bit on me. Mom rolled the cuffs under while reminding me I'd probably be wearing a sweater underneath it that would take up the slack. Besides, it needed to have *room to grow into,* just like any other purchase of clothing my mother would make for me. I looked at my reflection in the mirror. It looked perfect to me, dangling button and all. All that mattered was that it had waited for me and now it was *mine.*

I cradled my red beauty in my arms and headed towards the cashier's desk. My face was beaming as I imagined my new coat being placed onto the white tissue paper inside the trademark navy blue Lerner's box, and felt my fingers slip around the matching plastic handle as I carried my prized possession proudly out of the store. "How would you like to

Silence

pay for that today, ma'am?" posed the saleslady. "It will be a layaway," came my mother's reply. My smile faded like the sun being covered by a dark cloud. I kept one hand tenderly resting on the fabric while watching the woman fill out the necessary paperwork. In exchange for three dollars, my mother received the receipt and a schedule of payments. Reluctantly, I removed my hand from the coat. I insisted on watching as it was placed on a hanger, a copy of the bright yellow receipt with its bold black letters shouting *LAYAWAY* pinned to the front. There would be no tissue paper or trademark box after all, only a plastic bag draped over it.

It wasn't just my coat I left at Lerner's that afternoon. A silent piece of my heart stayed to keep it company while it waited for my return.

Chapter Eighteen

Sleeping with Jesus

It's amazing to me the things that our minds hold onto, put away for safekeeping in some invisible filing cabinet in our brains. Sometimes we can retrieve information within seconds; other times, we have to patiently wait...shifting through the backlog to find what we are looking for. Then, there are times when we aren't consciously searching at all – something we see or hear triggers the release of a long forgotten memory; or perhaps one that has been hidden away in the deep recesses of our minds. Once recalled, it can feel as real as the moment it happened – taking our breath away with either delight or despair – all in an instant. In writing this memoir, something I hadn't thought about for over fifty years came back with stunning recall.

Life was pretty run-of-the-mill when I was nine. My mother and I had settled down into a routine together. Each morning, after making me a breakfast of oatmeal or scrambled eggs and sending me off to school, she'd catch a bus downtown to go to

Silence

work. Employed as a cook at the Lincoln Inn, a small restaurant catering to locals, she'd be back by the time I got home from school. A homemade snack always greeted me as I walked in the door. The thought of biting into an oatmeal cookie, the warm chocolate nuggets melting in my mouth, hastened my trip to the bathroom to wash my hands – always a pre-requisite to sitting down at the table. As I drank my milk, my mother would indulge in a cup of tea along with our treats. Always interested in what I learned at school, my mother would listen intently as I spoke. Then she would tell me about her day; namely, what she cooked for the lunch special. My mother was a phenomenal cook – everyone thought so, especially her boss. Cooking for people made her happy.

One day, life threw us a curve ball. Walking home from school had been uneventful. Arriving home, I opened the back door, anticipating the familiar aroma of baking. I smelled nothing. The kitchen table was empty and things were uneasily quiet. With an unsteady feeling taking over my body, I called to my mother. Silence. Then, my Aunt Mary emerged from living room. Normally, I'd be pretty happy to see my mother's sister, but today her face looked tense. Always a straight shooter, my aunt cut to the chase. My mother had taken a fall at work and was in the hospital. Stunned, I felt the color drain from my face, as I shifted uneasily, feeling dizzy. Aunt Mary sat me down, assuring me things were not life threatening. I felt as if I were hearing her speak from under water as she explained that tests were being taken to find out the extent of my mother's

Sleeping with Jesus

injury. In the meantime, I'd need to spend the weekend at my grandmother's. Walking around in a daze, I found a paper shopping bag, and went upstairs to pack up some clothes and my toothbrush. Making sure I had my books to complete my homework assignments, I was as ready as I could be for what lay ahead.

My grandmother's house could be found in New Britain's "Little Italy," located on Franklin Street right next to Joe & Josephine's local grocery store. Joe would make fresh sausage every Thursday; the pungent aroma spilling out into the street as people went in and out. Entering the store, the tinkle of the bell on the door was always answered by a hearty hello from behind the meat counter. On Thursdays, everyone on the street paid the market a visit. Sometimes there would be a line out the door waiting. Joe knew each person's preference by heart – sweet or hot, and always put aside a pound of our favorite so we didn't have to wait in line. I loved visiting their store and can still imagine the sound of the squeaky floorboards under my feet, as I'd walk up and down the aisles, enchanted by the cramped contents on the shelves – olives, pasta in all shapes and sizes, marinated eggplant – -the food of my childhood. Staying with my grandmother always assured me a shiny dime to be spent on a coconut Italian ice. Josephine would dish out the treat. Sometimes, when I'd put my money on the old wooden counter, she would slide the dime back in my direction "for another time," she'd say with a knowing wink of her eye. They were a generous duo and the heart of neighborhood. Down the

Silence

street was the Mancini Packing Company. If you lived in the immediate vicinity, you never hung your wash out to dry on Wednesdays – unless you wanted your clothes to smell like the garlic-laden roasted peppers made at Mancini's. I'll never forget how delicious they were sandwiched in between two slices of warm homemade bread made by my grandmother's neighbor, a kindly old woman named Mrs. Margossi. Indeed, you can still buy them in stores today – some fifty years later – and they taste just like I remember.

My grandmother's house was fairly large but modest. Like many houses of its era, it was simple in structure, beginning with a few original rooms which my grandfather expanded to accommodate the needs of a growing family. I often imagined the rustic rock walls framing the small front lawn of the house as being the work of a neighborhood mason who would share stories of the old country with my aunts and uncles as he toiled. I still recall the beautiful red rose bushes lining the boundaries of the walls, their fragrance carried on the warm summer wind. My grandmother's roses were her pride and joy. Heaven forbid any kid's ball landing in one of her prized possessions. It would be banished to her "collection," a row of neatly placed trophies which sat on her porch. She believed it was a fair price to pay; it certainly kept the kids' wary of a repeat offense. Nonni, as I called her, was the consummate Italian grandmother. Anyone who came to visit would always leave well fed, dining on hearty and delicious ethnic dishes served up in her kitchen. Her spaghetti sauce was so good that you'd lap up every drop with

Sleeping with Jesus

your last hunk of bread, leaving your plate clean. Food was the center of her universe, along with going to church, of course.

St. Ann's was the Roman Catholic Church that every god-fearing Italian in her corner of New Britain attended. My grandmother was almost certainly their most devout member. Bright and early each day, she'd dress up, placing one of her favorite hats atop her short white hair. Off she'd go, making the pilgrimage to St. Ann's on foot. I can envision her making her way down the aisle to the front pew, shiny black vinyl pocketbook in the crook of her arm, rosary beads in hand. She was as reliable in her attendance as the parish priest who officiated the mass. To call her devout was more than an understatement. Her home contained statuary and religious artifacts to almost rival the church itself. Not to mention the many nuns in our family that would grace the presence of her living room when they were able to make a periodic visit away from the convent. I recall them sitting side-by-side on her sofa, a portrait in black and white, while the Last Supper hovered above them on the wall.

And so it was no surprise to me that upon my arrival at my grandmother's house that fateful weekend, that I found her sitting on her enclosed front porch, metal rocking chair creaking against the cement floor as she sat praying the rosary. This was the very first time I recall going to my grandmother's house without my mother. I felt like a boat lost at sea. Like a grand lighthouse, my nonni led me straight to the kitchen – to make me something to eat. In her world, food was the remedy

Silence

for fixing all your ills and the best way to your heart. We whiled away the time after supper sitting in front of the small black and white television as the bubbles heralding the start of the Lawrence Welk show filled the screen. I felt myself evaporate away just like one of them. My mother was my world, and I felt empty without her. The loud ring of the telephone startled both myself and my grandmother, her rosary beads dropping into her lap as she picked up the receiver. It was my Aunt Mary, with an update from the hospital. Although resting comfortably, my mother had suffered an injury to her back – a slipped disc. Her message to me was not to worry, she'd be home in a jiffy. For the next several minutes, my grandmother spoke to her daughter in Italian – leaving me to wonder if there was something they weren't telling me. The long-awaited call ended with the drop of the handset back into its cradle. My grandmother rose from her chair and headed down the hallway to the kitchen. Moments later she returned, carrying two cups of chamomile tea and biscotti to tide us over.

The inevitable arrived. It was time for me to go to bed. I took as long as I could to get into my pajamas. This delay served a two-fold purpose. I needed to cry without fuss, and prolong going to bed for as long as possible. My grandmother's voice – the broken English that was her vocal signature – resonated through the thick bathroom door. "Are you alright-a?" she asked with concern. Not wanting to cause her undue worry, I wiped the tears from my eyes; opened the door, and stepped out of my temporary sanctuary. Nonni began walking towards her

Sleeping with Jesus

bedroom, the shuffle of her slippers against the old linoleum in the hallway keeping time with the slight rocking of her aging body as she made her way. All too soon, we arrived at the threshold of her bedchamber which lay directly behind the living room. As she gently pushed the door open, a slow steady creak resounded. I kept my head lowered, my eyes looking down; there were things in this room I would rather not see. As I neared the bedside, I knew what was expected of me. Kneeling down on the small rug, I blessed myself and said my prayers under the watchful eye of both Christ and my grandmother. The coverlet for the bed had been neatly pulled down and folded at the foot of the bed. Crisp white pillow cases with embroidered edges cradled my head as I lay down. An almost guilty feeling overcame me as I settled down against the clean, ironed sheets, knowing they would soon give way to wrinkles. My grandmother bent over me; and, with one quick snap tucked the sheets in between the mattress and box spring. With a kiss on my forehead and a quick pinch to my cheeks, she turned to leave. "Goodnight-a, sleep-tight-a," were her parting words as she closed the door behind her, the long, tired squeal of its hinges the last sound I heard before the stillness set in.

I lay there immobilized in between the stiff sheets, my arms pinned at my sides. Part of me wanted to move – the other part felt somehow comforted in this odd cocoon. Although I wasn't sleepy, I kept my eyes closed tight – I knew what sight would greet me should I gaze towards the wall next to me. I lay still and quiet, my breath shallow. The darkness of the room

Silence

enveloped me as the distinct sensation of not quite being alone overtook me. From within the ornate frames on the bureaus, the old-fashioned photographs with the blank eyes of relatives long in their graves pierced the blackness. Alive once again and staring at me, I felt their presence in the room. Something deep inside willed me to open my eyes and look into the void. The room felt alive as my eyes acclimated to the darkness; shadows emerged outlining the statues of saints forever frozen in time. In my heightened sense of loneliness, I felt overwhelmed with claustrophobic fear. I closed my eyes and began to tap my fingers against my legs, willing myself to breathe. All fell silent except for the beating of my heart, its thumping both felt and heard. From within the quiet came the sudden compulsion to open my eyes once again. Drawn by some unseen force, my gaze began the slow ascent up the wall on the side of the bed. My heart began to race as form became apparent. A single ray of light from the streetlamp pierced the darkness finding its mark upon the wall, illuminating the life-size face of the crucified Christ. The plaster cast countenance glowed eerily, its features depicting the intensity of the moment just prior to death. The pale white face drained of all color – its pained lips parted as if to release one last breath leered down at me. The forehead pierced by a jagged crown of thorns – its sharp points laden with crimson drops of blood, threatened to drip onto the crisp white sheets below. My eyes were riveted on the imploring brown eyes of the Son of God, feeling them penetrate my very soul. In slow motion, I watched as His eyes came alive – blinking once, twice…never breaking contact with mine. A

Sleeping with Jesus

teardrop formed and slowly trickled down a cheek, mixing with a drop of blood as it made its descent. My breath caught as I watched the tear fall onto the taut sheet. I felt as if I were in a silent movie – vivid yet fragmented. Not a sound came from my throat…not a word escaped. Wide eyes unblinking, I stared upwards once again. The tragic face, suspended forever in time, hung motionless against the fading wallpaper. Suddenly, my body felt like lead, as I sunk into the mattress. Exhausted from fear, my mind ceased to function. I fell into that space of silence deep within as my eyes closed, the image slowly fading away.
I was sleeping with Jesus.

Chapter Nineteen

Farewell Lancaster Drive

Our lives took a big detour in 1963, following my mother's accident. A traumatic fall at her workplace had spawned the need for surgery to my mother's back for a slipped disc. My Aunt Mary had been dispatched to retrieve me, bringing me to my grandmother's house where I would stay during my mom's initial hospitalization. While Mary and her sister, Connie, looked and sounded eerily identical, to most people my aunt came across with an aloof personality – the opposite of my mother. Mary, who was born in 1913, had left New Britain behind for the big city, New York, at a time when women didn't do that sort of thing. Fiercely independent, as a young woman she worked as a waitress making her own way. I was always a little leery of her when I was young, she felt formidable. Still, she was always kind to me; just a bit gruff, as if she was uncomfortable with kids. Now, here I was spending the weekend with my grandmother and her, in the house where the sisters grew up along with the rest of their siblings.

Farewell Lancaster Drive

It was always a bit of a culture shock to go from the familiarity of the projects where I had grown up to the old-fashioned Italian neighborhood of Franklin Street. My grandparents had come from Naples and raised their family, along with other immigrants, in this small enclave. People here knew each other very well, they had grown together through good, flourishing times and sustained one another through turbulent times including the deaths of loved ones. News of my mother's injury was out on the grapevine, no doubt very soon after it occurred. Even though we didn't live in the neighborhood, inherently she was still part of it. Taking a walk with my grandmother to Joe's Red & White Store, just a few houses away, elicited old women's questions and commentary about Connie's well-being as we walked by their porches where they sat on their rocking chairs, crocheting or cooling off with a cold lemonade. Every voice was heard, as we stopped momentarily to engage in conversation along the way. There was no hurrying to the store; it took a full fifteen minutes to travel what could have taken three minutes. Franklin Street reflected life lived in the moment; and, there was always enough time to share it.

My mother's surgery had taken place on Friday and went well; she would be recovering in the hospital for about a week. Since I still had school to attend, Aunt Mary decided she would pack a bag and spend the week at our house while her sister was on the mend. It was strange being with her for those seven days. She looked enough like my mother to elicit looks from some of the neighbors, who would shake their heads in disbelief when

Silence

they realized it wasn't Connie. Hearing her call me from the kitchen when it was time to eat always unnerved me, as I'd find myself responding "OK, Mom" so similar were their voices.

The days without her passed by slowly, one blending into the next. I missed my mother tremendously. We had our rituals – morning and night – things that had formed the fabric of our life together. Without her everything seemed out of sync. Even with Aunt Mary's company, I felt lonely. Somehow her close resemblance to Connie simultaneously brought me both comfort and made me melancholy. Luckily, school took up most of the day distracting me from my thoughts. One afternoon I came home to find my mother in the living room, resting. Her presence made me realize what a hole in my heart her absence had caused. I was thrilled to have her back where she belonged – the smile on my face welcomed her home. Now things could get back to normal again. But that was not to be. While the surgery was considered a success; thereafter, my mother would always have to walk with the aid of a cane. Our whole world suddenly changed. She was no longer able to continue working as a cook, being unable to stand for any considerable length of time. That felt like small potatoes compared with the fact that climbing a flight of stairs was definitely out of the question. This meant my mother could no longer navigate the two floor duplex that was the only home I had ever known. My world came crashing in on me, as the realization that we would have to move took hold. *Where would we go? How could we leave? What would happen to us?* My ten-year-old brain bombarded me with more

Farewell Lancaster Drive

questions than answers. The pronouncement was made post haste. We would be moving to my grandmother's house where a small three-room addition awaited us. In a matter of a few short weeks, Franklin Street would become our new address.

When the dust settled from the news, I was heartsick. This meant that I would be leaving "him." I could not remember a day without his presence. Rainy days brightened up when I'd see his smile. I felt butterflies bouncing around in my stomach as if they were trying valiantly to exit their cocoon. This couldn't be happening, but it was, and I couldn't stop it. David, a year older than me, shared my birth month and my heart. Destiny had brought us together when we moved to the projects. The stage was set at a pretend "tea party" held in the living room, while our moms had coffee in the adjoining dining room. His mother, "Little Abbie," as she was affectionately called, would become my mother's best friend; and, I would fall in love with her son. While it seems implausible to acknowledge one could love at such an early age, I assure you it was true. In fact, the feeling remained with me throughout my young life. There was something about David, even then, that defied explanation. While we all played together as kids, he was always on the periphery of things. He didn't quite fit in with everyone; still, the two of us were naturally comfortable together. We shared the unspoken language of children who recognize something of themselves in each other that draws them close. *Somehow, innately, we knew similar experiences had befallen us – we were kindred spirits.* Suddenly, this was all coming to an end.

Silence

How could it? Franklin Street seemed like a million miles away, it might as well have been the other side of the world.

It had been raining on and off on the fateful day when our "stuff" was packed into a waiting truck, leaving the rooms we had lived in bare and lifeless. Teary goodbyes had been said to Barry, Mark, Ann, and even Katie. It was all a blur. The saving grace in all of this would be that Little Abbie was going to drive us to our new home; best of all, David would be coming along. *In the midst of having to leave everything familiar, there was a silver lining after all.* It was time – we got into the car – the two of us sat next to each other in the back compartment of the old station wagon. Looking out the rear window, my neighborhood slowly began to disappear. We had just barely left the boundaries of the project when the clouds returned, reclaiming their earlier gift. Out of the blue, David shouted to his mother to stop the car. She pulled over. He said he changed his mind and wanted to stay home after all. His mother asked the reason – none was forthcoming. He was adamant; she gave in. As he climbed over the back seat towards his escape, he looked back. I swore there were tears in his blue eyes. One thing is certain, it was raining in my heart as I said goodbye to Lancaster Drive.

Chapter Twenty

The Voice from the Cellar and the Open Window

I can recall our bedroom on Franklin Street completely when I close my eyes. A small square of a room, it was loaded with mismatched hand-me-down furniture. Our twin four poster mahogany beds stood side by side like silent sentinels. I polished them regularly with spray-on Pledge to keep them shiny. Although they were a junk store find, I knew they were my mother's pride and joy. The bed closest to the door belonged to my mother. Mine was squeezed into the remaining space, a small nightstand wedged into the space between them. A pot-bellied lamp along with a supply of Hall's menthol eucalyptus cough drops sat atop the table. Two bureaus that clearly had seen better days stood straight and tall, looming over me as I slept no more than an arm's width away. The close proximity to my bed allowed their drawers to open no more than halfway. Luckily, I was able to squeeze my skinny hand inside to pull out any contents.

Silence

What we used as a closet could have doubled as a refrigerator, cut out as it were into part of an unheated porch which my grandmother used to store food. Instead of a door, we put up double blankets in the winter months to keep the cold out. Along the ceiling of the room, there was a small, roughly-cut rectangle that allowed the heat from the gas stove in the kitchen to filter through. This was my mother's idea to allow the heat to circulate in our three-room cold flat. While it never quite worked as well as one would hope, my mother always tried her best to improvise. Rather than a door separating the living room from the bedroom, she had jerry-rigged a heavy curtain between the rooms, affording some privacy when I went to bed. My nightly ritual of checking under my bed and diligently making the sign of the cross on all four sides of my mattress gave me a false sense of security, but I carried it out just the same. I'd drift off to sleep listening to the drone of the television, knowing my mother was just on the other side, no doubt crocheting potholders or the like; her hands were never idle. Hours later, I'd awaken slightly hearing the familiar creak of the bed as she climbed into the bed next to mine, adjusting pillows and blankets until all fell quiet. This was always short-lived, as my mother had asthma and her breathing was often loud and erratic. Unnerving at first, I had grown used to it. It was for me a kind of comforting white noise in its own odd way. Drifting back to deep sleep, this became the ritual of sharing a room with my mother.

The Voice from the Cellar and the Open Window

Other nights would be different. Those were the ones I learned to dread. I introduced a form of self-talk to keep myself calm when the voice would start. Penetrating my subconscious with its intrusion, it always started as the very softest of whispers, challenging my ears to detect and decipher the words being spoken, however elusive they were. I would try to tell myself that it was just the voice from the television set, but I knew better. There was an eerie quality to the sound that ran chills down my spine, making me pull my covers up closer around my neck. Sometimes I'd curl myself up, drawing my knees up so tightly under my nightgown, I could hardly breathe. At first the voice was always impossible to make out. But, just in that moment when I had myself convinced that I was only hearing things – that it was only the active mind of a child working overtime – it would call my name.

Without skipping a beat, next would come the scratching, the sound of fingernails being slowly pulled down a wooden door. All the while, my name was repeated over and over again, each syllable drawled out in a deep, painful whisper, trailing off into a mere wisp of sound. My mind was fragmented in fear as I tried to keep myself from imagining just what was behind the door and; worst of all, what it wanted.

I had learned that calling out to my mother was futile. The very moment that I did, all would become still and quiet. She would come into the room, listening intently for some version of what her frightened child had described, but hearing nothing. A cup of hot milk was readied, laden with honey, something

Silence

to ease me out of my apparent nightmare and settle me back to sleep. She'd leave the room when I had finished the last sip, content that it would do the trick. After a few moments, I'd find myself becoming sleepy, eyes fluttering open every now and then, until finally surrendering to their increasing heaviness. It was there, in that space between wakefulness and slumber that I would begin to relax, thawing my frozen terror-filled body within the cradling warmth of the blankets surrounding me. Drifting deeper into sleep, I recall willing myself to replace niggling fears with thoughts that brought me comfort. As I filled my mind with thoughts of my beloved cats, I found tranquility at last.

Somewhere in the vast reaches of my unconsciousness, I would hear my mother join me in the bed next to mine, the familiarity of the creaking of the mattress springs and the inevitable sounds of her breathing assuring me that I was not alone. In the stillness of the twilight place where we are uncertain if we are awake or merely dreaming, I became somehow aware of my heartbeat. I could hear its rhythm thrumming steadily yet faintly, its echo drawing me toward a state of pre-wakefulness. As my consciousness slowly returned I realized that it was not my heartbeat at all, but the sound of something tapping on my windowpane. It would have been nice to have had the luxury of convincing myself that the sound was that of a tree branch moving in the wind. I knew better. The narrow outdoor passageway dividing our rooms from my grandmother's part of the house left no room for such an option. I could feel

The Voice from the Cellar and the Open Window

myself swallowing harder and harder as this recognition was confirmed, seeing the hand sliding slowly across the top of the window pane its outline made visible by the dim light behind it. Praying silently that I was only dreaming, I was jolted further into wakefulness as the window slowly began to slide open. My voice failed me as I tried to call out to my mother, only a chirp amidst her deep slumbering snore. My eyes felt as if they were pinned open, all sensation of blinking gone, as I watched the hand reach through the window; deliberately pausing as if its owner relished my mounting terror. It was then that every cell in my body vibrated itself into a scream, my mother bolting upright hearing it pierce her slumber to its core.

Immediately calling to me, she turned on the small lamp on the nightstand, the sudden light chasing away the darkness and the intruder simultaneously. In between shaky breaths, I rattled out my story for my mother. As she held me close, her finger pointed to the window. I followed the unmarked trail with my eyes. To my confusion and disbelief, the window was closed. Her words were working furiously to eradicate the fear within me, willing me to understand that I had only been dreaming. Wanting desperately to create a feeling of safety and sanctuary for me, she went to the window to lock it. It was then I watched the color drain from my mother's face, as she saw the imprint of a hand left behind on the glass.

Looking back from this vantage point, some fifty years later, I don't know which was scarier for my mother: thinking it was an actual intruder or embracing the possibility that it

Silence

was the madness that lurked within her son. I know it gave me no great comfort when it became evident that it was my own brother who was responsible for the ghostly voice emanating from behind the cellar door. Junior's psychotic enactments were both the waking and dreaming nightmares of my life. My earliest remembrances began around age four and followed me throughout elementary school. Chock full of episodes befitting a good horror story, they are shared without the need for embellishment. They set the stage for my natural curiosity to be replaced with timidity. Junior had successfully programmed fear so deep within me that sometimes his mere commentary about something that might happen to me would set me reeling. His uncanny ability to convince people that it wasn't him perpetrating events – even in the face of staggering evidence – left me second-guessing myself and breeding an innate lack of self-confidence within me.

Chapter Twenty-One

The Attic

I can feel the apprehension building in my body just thinking about telling this story. I used to absolutely hate having to go up into the attic in our house on Franklin Street. I never voluntarily went up there. In fact, I'd do everything I could do to avoid it, but sometimes I just couldn't get away with having to climb those stairs. I instinctively knew when my mother was going to ask me to either go get something or to put something up in the attic. I tried to avoid coming in contact with her because I hated to refuse her, knowing she couldn't climb stairs with her bad back. Sooner or later she'd catch up with me and I knew that I'd be making the trip.

There was only one way I would do this. My mother would have to stand at the bottom of those stairs and talk to me the entire time it took me to walk up fourteen steps to the landing, reaching the door to the attic on the second floor. I remember counting every step, hearing the click of my shoe on the little metal tread on each stair. I watched my hand turning

Silence

progressively whiter as I clutched the wooden railing, willing it to support me as it creaked underneath my death-like grip. As always, I would try to focus my eyes to look down at my feet instead of at the top of the stairway. Somehow, they would betray me, pulled by some invisible string to gaze upwards into the black, vacant eyes of my mother's dead sister, Lucy. The sad portrait of the beautiful four-year-old child standing all alone, plaid dress with white starched collar and big white bow perched perilously atop her head made me lose the ability to breathe. Her eyes would stare into mine, freezing me in my tracks. Lucy, who looked remarkably like my mother, had died of scarlet fever. There was no cure at the time of her childhood. All that was left of her was this one solitary glimpse.

Once on the small landing in front of the door that was the gateway to my fear, I would always hesitate and swallow so hard that it hurt. Looking back over my shoulder at my mom to make sure she was at the bottom of the stairs, I'd put my skinny finger haltingly through the knothole that served as a doorknob and flick open the hook-and-eye lock that kept the door closed. My teeth would clench in a grimace as my foot gave the bottom of the door a slight kick, loosening the casing's grip on the aged wood. The door would swing open slowly with a creak that sent chills up my spine every time. My mother's voice would seem farther and farther away as the rising tide of the sound of my own pulse pounded through my ears. The next part was always the hardest, taking that first step into the darkness. It felt like it took an eternity before I was able to convince myself to start

The Attic

the process of going into the abyss. Somewhere in the back of my mind, I knew my mother was telling me that it was okay and that she was right there. It didn't count for much. The only thing that I could do was remind myself that I knew that it took exactly twenty-nine steps to move through the dark space that was the entry and reach the next room.

Time stood still as I willed my feet to move forward. Each footstep made the floorboards cry out in what sounded like agony to my child's mind. I always kept my arms pinned to my sides so I wouldn't touch anything. I dreaded moving through a cobweb, remembering how the sticky threads of its design stuck to my arm on my last visit, making me feel like a snared insect waiting for the inevitable ghastly spider to return to its prey. As I finally reached the opening to the room where the promise of light awaited, I found myself talking out loud, my voice taking the place of my mother's which had grown quiet. In a state of suspended animation, I'd take a deep breath. The dry dead air filled my lungs, its musty scent sticking in my nostrils. Steadying myself, I would slide my right hand carefully around the corner of the splintering door jamb onto the wall. Feeling my way upwards, I gingerly moved my fingers, crawling up inch-by-inch along the crumbling wallpaper until I felt the cold metal of the beaded pull chain to the bare light bulb that was my salvation.

One day, I made what was to be my last trip to the attic. It followed pretty much the same scenario with a twist that included my brother and me being the only two people home

Silence

at the time. Somehow, he convinced me to go up to the attic; the details as to how he did this escape me. He was a natural born con-artist and could always find a way to manipulate me into doing his bidding. Given his natural talents in this realm, I know now that as an innocent, I stood no chance. Junior stood at the bottom of the stairwell, as promised, stoic as a watchful soldier guarding his charge, as I began my ascent. His voice was utterly calm and reassuring, each measured phrase matching the cadence of my footsteps, lulling me like a siren's song to open the door to an unknowable hell. Once through the door, breathlessly counting the twenty-nine steps I knew would bring me out of the darkness, I reached for the pull chain. I felt nothing. My fingers already beginning to twitch and tremble, I inched them up higher still. Nothing. In the small space in time allotted to heed the inner call to stop and turn around, I hesitated. One more try. Relief! The chain was only twisted up around the fixture. My mind felt reassured. I gave it a hearty pull, half expecting it to break off in my hand. No light. The undeniable creaking of a heavy door being closed behind me. Darkness blacker than I could have imagined encompassed me, as the dim light that had filtered in from outside of the attic disappeared. I screamed out my brother's name. I heard silence. I froze with the panic of entrapment. Only twenty-nine steps to reach the door. My ten-year-old mind lost its bearings. I began to run my hands along the wall, feeling its rough plaster crumble under my fingertips as I inched my way towards the door. I felt like I was moving in slow motion, unable to go any faster until my hands felt the thick, wet ooze – a product of my

The Attic

brother's demented mind – spread between my fingers and slide down my wrists. Catapulted by a fear I'd never known, I found the door. Like a bolt of white lightning, the adrenaline rushing through my veins carried me down the stairs my feet barely touching a step. Screaming my brother's name, I ran through the house. Stone cold silence was the response.

No one was home.

Chapter Twenty-Two

Little Miss Responsibility

Sometimes I think I was born responsible. I certainly grew up feeling pretty serious about most things. When people talk about how they wish they were kids again – the fun they had, the vacations with their families, riding bikes, going to summer camp, swimming in their backyard pool - I reserve comment. Fun is not the word that I necessarily use to describe my childhood. It was not the mainstay of being a kid for me. Vacations away from home? Non-existent. One or two summers, I did get to go spend a week in the neighboring town of Southington visiting my cousin, who was a few years older than me. Since our neighborhood was populated mainly by boys when I lived on Franklin Street, it was refreshing to be around a girl, and I was especially fond of her. We connected, we shared secrets. My cousin was responsible for doing all of the chores around the house and taking care of her brother. Our extracurricular activity consisted mainly of taking walks, squeezed in between the multitude of things on her to-do list assigned by her mother. Still, it was a change of scenery, and

Little Miss Responsibility

I welcomed being in her presence in much the same way she looked forward to my visit. It was a brief respite for both of us.

Between lack of proximity to other girls in my neighborhood and my overall shyness, my mother became my best friend and I her right hand. The debilitating injury she had suffered to her back made her unable to walk long distances. As walking was our main mode of transportation around town, this really impacted her ability to take care of the basic necessities that required attention, such as grocery shopping, picking up her prescriptions, and bill paying. I became her two good legs, and our ability to be self-sufficient rested heavily on my shoulders.

I had a rather slight build growing up which earned me the nickname "Boney Maroney." To make things easier for me, we invested in the purchase of a folding grocery cart. It was money well spent since carrying bags of food and supplies would have been considerably more difficult without it. Every Wednesday, my mom and I would write up the shopping list together. It always included the Stop 'n Save special – a three-pound package of ground beef that cost $1.59. It became meatloaf, meatballs, hamburgers, Salisbury steak, chili for hotdogs, and some rather imaginative other dishes my mother would concoct – all of them delicious given their humble beginning. I took getting groceries pretty seriously; with our meager food budget it was a necessity. I knew how to take advantage of shopping the day-old bin for bread or muffins, and always found the vegetables that had been set-aside for quick sale when they were considered less than perfect. Overripe tomatoes

Silence

readily became homemade spaghetti sauce. Bananas that were soft were ideal for banana bread. Bruised peppers were perfect for stuffing. The cashiers got to know me, and always chuckled when I loaded up the conveyor belt with all the "specials," pointing out that I knew how to stretch a dollar like a rubber band. When Harry, the bagger, had filled my grocery cart up with paper sacks, he would give me a friendly wink as I thanked him for packing. I would then wait patiently for my receipt and the coveted S & H Green Stamps we'd earn for every dollar spent. At home, I'd paste them into the stamp book, anticipating the day when the book would be full. Mom and I would save up a multitude of them, then pull out the Sperry & Hutchinson catalog to see what we could trade them in for. I remember after diligently saving for the better part of a year, we traded in our five books of stamps for a new great toaster!

Grocery shopping completed, I passed through the automatic doors, pulling my cart behind me as I headed home. Listening to the sound of the wheels thumping over the cracks in the sidewalk, I'd look into the windows of the storefronts as I passed by. On hot days, if they didn't have customers, shopkeepers might be seen in the doorways keeping cool. We greeted each other with pleasantries, most of them commenting how lucky my mother was to have such a responsible daughter to count on.

Once I got past the shops, my spirit sank as the landscape changed significantly. Without the buzz of people around, the vacant lots I needed to pass by became ominous. Sometimes

Little Miss Responsibility

I would be startled by a voice coming out from a darkened doorway of one of the boarded up buildings. "Hey, little girlie, whatcha got in that cart of yours?" a grubby looking man would quiz. *Never answer, ignore him, just keep walking* – I'd hear the watchwords my mother had taught me. I'd scurry away like a little scared rabbit, usually to the echo of laughter behind me. After that, my pace would remain pretty quick, cutting down on the amount of time it took me to reach the railroad crossing signaling the turn that would bring me back to civilization. First passing the gas station, then the lumberyard, I would reach the last leg of my trek. Twenty minutes and I was home, my precious cargo intact.

Once a month, I would be entrusted to pay the bills and pick up my mother's prescription at the local downtown pharmacy. On that Saturday morning, we'd sit at the kitchen table together after breakfast. From inside a well-worn brown accordion folder, my mother would pull out the used number ten envelopes which were clearly marked: light bill, phone bill, and gas bill. I can still see her handwriting on the right-hand corner of each one as clear as day. She would lay out each statement on the table and paper clip some cash on top of each one. Then, one after another, she gingerly placed them into their respective envelopes. Into my shoulder strap pocketbook, they would go for safekeeping. As I put them in, I would always double-check to make sure they were all accounted for before I snapped it shut securely. Then, I'd make certain the snap was closed tightly. *Couldn't be too careful.*

Silence

    I always followed the same route when it came to bill-paying day. First stop, Connecticut Light and Power. The massive glass doors with their long silver handles were tough to navigate, but I would usually be able to follow somebody in or sneak through when someone was on their way out. Although I knew the way by heart, I'd follow the yellow tape on the floor to the area where the customer service people took payments. A massive black marble counter that easily spanned twenty feet stood between me and the four cashiers. I waited dutifully behind the velvet rope for my turn. When it came, I'd make my approach, trying to make eye contact with the lady behind the glass. Standing on my tippy toes, I'd slide my envelope in her direction through the slot. She opened it and counted out the bills attached to the clip, then she'd recount them. "There's not enough money in here, you need five more dollars," came her brisk comment, with a roll of her eyes to further make her point. "It's what we have, please put it on account," I responded meekly. It was never easy to speak those words, although I'd delivered this line more than once before. "Well, you really should try to pay the entire amount." There was no reply needed. I just waited as she stamped the statement and sent it back through the window. "May I have my envelope back, please?" I hesitantly asked. She reached down for a moment, likely retrieving it from her trash basket, and unceremoniously pushed it my way. Putting it back in my purse, I turned to leave, red-faced with embarrassment as I walked past the other people in line.

Little Miss Responsibility

I was dreading the next stop, knowing that I would encounter pretty much the same thing. We never quite had enough cash to cover all three bills. Mom alternated which one could receive the entire payment each month. I loved hearing the polite "thank you," as the smiling cashier slid the lucky statement emblazoned with *paid in full* in my direction.

Today I had one last stop, Center Pharmacy on the green, to pick up my mom's asthma prescription. Sometimes I thought that she needed her inhaler more than she used it, trying to dole it out sparingly to get through the month. There were times when that didn't work and she'd need an early refill. That meant extra money. Connie had made an arrangement with the pharmacy to run a tab if we didn't have the cash available. When my turn at the counter came, I asked for the prescription and waited. The cashier rang it up and asked for payment. "Please put it on my mother's tab," I said with a polite smile. "I'm sorry, I can't," came the reply. "There must be a mistake, my mother called the pharmacist before," I answered trying to sound confident. "What seems to be the problem?" spoke the owner of the pharmacy, as I recognized his familiar face. When he saw me standing there bewildered and holding up the line for his other customers, he asked me to step aside. "I need my mother's medicine, and she won't give it to me," I pleaded, not understanding what was happening. "You need to tell your mother that she needs to pay the balance on her account before she can get another prescription filled here," the emotionless face spoke, saying the words I couldn't fathom

Silence

as he turned away. Instinctively, I reached out and pulled his arm, bravely making my plea, "Please, you don't understand, she can't breathe without it!" He tried to keep moving, but I loudly repeated myself, as if he must not have heard me the first time. Hearing him trying to repeat what he had said before brought on spasms and a crying jag I couldn't control, behavior that was unlike me, born of my responsibility for my mother's well-being. His face reddened immediately as he met the eyes of other customers staring at him and the little girl who stood before him practically begging for her mother's lifeline. "Okay, okay, don't cry!" he hurriedly said, and grabbed the small white bag off the counter, handing it over to me as he muttered his earlier edict again under his breath. I swallowed hard and took it before he could change his mind. I ran out of the store, never looking back. That day in the pharmacy, at the tender age of eleven, I had done what my mother could not. I had paid in full all by myself.

Chapter Twenty-Three

The Girl Scout Uniform

Thinking back on so many memories as I am writing this book, it's amazing to me how many details I am beginning to recall. Things long forgotten, or more accurately, buried, are being given a chance to bubble up within me and make their way to the surface. My memories are beginning to breathe within me, coming alive from the silence. The irony of it all is that for the first time in my sixty-two years, I've taken a three-day sabbatical – alone – to come to this place within myself. I'd been in stall mode for quite some time in my writing, primarily because for me when "duty calls," I answer. I must admit that in the course of writing this book, life threw me some curve balls; and, I felt compelled to sideline my efforts. However, my innate creativity has allowed me poetic license with the definition of "duty," thereby replacing it several times with what may actually be more accurately described as distraction.

Silence

Getting back to the concept of duty, I can't help but recall my days as a Girl Scout. Raising our right hands, three fingers held together with thumb and baby finger touching, our troop would solemnly recite: "On my honor, I will try to serve God and my country, to help people at all times, and to live by the Girl Scout Law." These words were meant to be taken seriously. The year was 1964 and I was eleven years old. Sometimes I felt like I was born responsible, so scouting should have been a good fit, since being part a troop appeared to necessitate such an admirable trait. Unfortunately for me, it was the "fitting in" part where things went awry.

We had moved less than a year before from the projects where I grew up, and were now living in my grandmother's house in the Italian part of New Britain – the same house where my mother and her siblings grew up. I had left all familiarity behind. We needed to move when my mother injured her back and could no longer climb stairs. Although the Franklin Street neighborhood kids were friendly enough, any way you looked at it, I was still shy and spent most of my time alone.

To try and remedy the situation, my mother – bless her heart – came up with the brilliant idea of starting a Girl Scout troop of her own, thereby ensuring I could participate without feeling too shy to join. Unlike my mother who could strike up a conversation with anyone, I found it more than difficult to talk with people I didn't know. She could also sew up a storm without the need for patterns and create craft projects from almost anything on hand – all the makings of a good Girl Scout

The Girl Scout Uniform

leader back then. So it was that with these tools in hand, my mother became the proud leader of Troop #4 at my elementary school.

One would have thought that with my mother as the leader, I'd feel right at home, and that Girl Scout meetings would be something I'd look forward to. I did, at first. Although the other girls in the troop seemed to enjoy my mother's company more than mine, I didn't begrudge them a moment. I was quite used to being on the sidelines. Regrettably, what started out a well-meaning idea turned out to be the bane of my life during sixth grade – all because of a uniform. My mother had not initially realized that both she and I would be required to wear an "official" uniform. Alas, that was the rule. Because money was tight, there was no way this was in the cards. Always good with a creative solution, my mother made herself a green dress in the "correct" color, thereby saving a good deal of money. My guess was the Girl Scout Council allowed this discrepancy in adhering to the rules to take place mainly because scout leaders were hard to come by, and they knew they had a great deal with my mother. There would be no exception for me, however - I'd need a uniform. My mother presented me with a surprise one day after school, handing me a box tied with a green ribbon that showed signs of having been "ironed out". My mother found a way to reuse everything, including the wrapping paper which had clearly seen better days. None of the outside trappings really mattered. I was enthralled with seeing what was inside. I opened the box to see a touch of green peering out from the wrinkled tissue paper. Lying underneath it, folded perfectly, was my very own Girl Scout uniform. I admired it for a moment, noticing that it looked almost new! I turned to my mother who was all smiles, as she pulled my aunt's camera out from behind her back and told me to go try it on so we could take some pictures. My mother absolutely loved taking photographs of every momentous event, and this clearly qualified. I gave her a big hug and kiss and was off to the bedroom to try it on.

As soon as I pulled it out of the box, my excitement fizzled like a flat bottle of soda. It was huge. I didn't want to put it on but I knew I had to; my mother was waiting to immortalize this moment on film. I unbuttoned the front slowly, dreading putting it on. As I pulled it over my head, it flopped down onto my tiny shoulders, hanging on my body like a sack. My boney arms and legs dangled from beneath it as I looked down at myself. In my mind, I looked horrid and felt worse. My mother's voice was coaxing me to come out so she could see how I looked. I half-smiled as I came out from behind the curtain that served as a door to our shared bedroom. There was no way I was going to hurt my mother's feelings. I knew that she must have gone to great lengths to get the money for this uniform. Truth be told, most of my clothes were ill-fitting because they were always meant to have "room to grow into" and never fit quite right on my small frame. As I walked out into the living room, my mother quickly came over and tied a dark green grosgrain ribbon around my waist – adjusting the fit by scrunching the

The Girl Scout Uniform

excess fabric around until evenly distributed. Apparently, there wasn't enough cash to afford the fancy woven green belt with the metal closure featuring the Girl Scout insignia on it, so my mother had improvised. I willed myself to follow my mother outdoors and, after prompting me how to pose, she snapped two photos – just in case one didn't come out. Back in those days, you had to have film developed so you always took an "extra" of momentous occasions as an insurance policy of sorts.

When the day of our next meeting arrived, I had to wear my uniform to school, as was the custom back then, since our troop's meeting was held right after school in the gymnasium. I woke up to find it freshly starched and pressed on a hanger waiting for me. There was no way out of wearing it, so off I went to school. My eyes averted everyone on the playground at school as we waited in line for the school bell to ring and the doors to open. I tried my best to ignore the cruel commentary comparing my uniform to the rest of the girls in my troop – all dressed to perfection right down to the official belt. Jokes were being made about *how many girl scouts could fit into my uniform.* Laughter resounded as the answer – *the whole troop* – was blurted out by one of the kids. I sat through school all day, sinking down into my chair trying to hide my uniform – all to no avail. Going to the actual meeting was even worse, as my troop members were giggling and finger-pointing at me whenever my mother turned her back. I didn't have the heart to tell her what was going on. I knew my mother meant well, she was just trying to get "the most bang for the buck," as she

Silence

called it - this uniform was meant to last throughout my girl scouting years.

I persevered in Troop #4 for an entire school year of meetings – my rationale being to get some use out of the outfit, given my mother's attempt at scouting was primarily for my benefit. The two photographs capturing me in my official uniform have survived the years. Looking at them as I write these words, the old adage *a picture is worth a thousand words* comes to mind. My embarrassment is clearly evident beneath an attempt to smile, the real me disappearing behind the fabric. I never grew into that uniform – only out of it.

Chapter Twenty-Four

Buon Natale

Growing up in an Italian household, Christmas was a true mix of celebrating the birth of Jesus and festivities centered around decorating the house in preparation for the holiday. My grandmother would spend a good deal of time at church being the rather devout Roman Catholic she was. However, she doled out equal time to making sure the house was adorned appropriately. What did that mean exactly? Well, in my grandmother's eyes, it signaled time to pull out the big cardboard box slumbering in the attic, dust it off, and haul it downstairs to her living room. She would ready the space next to the television set in preparation, moving the magazine rack to another place and pushing her big chair a little bit more into the room to create space for her tree. Her daughters Mary and Connie would do the honors, opening the box and putting together the branches one by one until it shone in all its silver glory. Indeed, this six-foot-tall aluminum tree was her pride and joy. Decorated with a themed single color ornament, it waited for her to add the pièce de résistance - the coveted color

Silence

wheel. How she loved sitting in her chair watching the tree turn from gold to green, then blue to red, never tiring of the endless cavalcade of color.

My mother and I had a much different tradition when it came to *our* tree. We always had the real deal. Emphasis on the *deal*. There was a place that sold beautiful evergreens down on the corner right before St. Andrew's Church. They'd set up light bulbs high overhead to show off their wares as the first of December arrived. Passing by on the way to my friend's house, I would slow down to savor the pine scent that filled the air as I imagined which tree would find its way to our house. It would be a bit of a wait before that happened - Christmas Eve, to be exact. The afternoon of December 24th, I would get out the old wooden sled that stood just inside the shed in our tiny backyard in anticipation of getting our tree. Together, my mother and I would make the trek to the corner of Dwight Street, her cane providing the balance she required to navigate the packed down snow. Nonetheless, it took a while to get there as we took it slow as a cautionary measure. The time passed as we sang our favorite carols along the way. By the time we finished singing *Chestnuts Roasting on an Open Fire,* we had arrived. The smell of pine welcomed us, although the lot was almost empty. A man stood before an old barrel, keeping his hands warm over the fire. With a quick nod as a hello, we perused the lot. My mom spotted a tree that she thought was perfect, with a good number of branches evenly spaced, and no big gaps anywhere. The guy came over, noting to us that she'd picked out a beauty,

Buon Natale

and held out his hand for the five-dollar bill it would cost. The negotiation started, and my mother gave her bid: "Could you knock it down to two bucks? After all, it's Christmas Eve." He muttered something about already shaving off a few dollars, and didn't want to budge on the price. "What else you got?" came my mother's inquiry, and he quickly shot back his retort, "For two bucks? Not much." We all stood there motionless, a stand-off of sorts. The guy kept looking from me to my mother and back again, then he kicked the toe of his boot into the small snowbank next to him in resignation, giving in with an "Alright, already; I got something I guess." He went back to the far corner of the lot and dragged back a tree. He shook off the snow and held it out for my mother's inspection. It was pretty good on one side and fairly sparse on the other. I knew my mother's thought process. She'd put the tree in the corner to hide its faults and make the most of it. I nearly choked when I heard my mother's audacious offer: "I'll give you a dollar for it, since it's really half a tree!" Silence filled the pine scented space. He considered, looking at her raised eyebrow as she stood her ground. I could see him softening up. "Take the tree and have a Merry Christmas," was all he said as he turned back to the fire.

Once again, my mother proved her ability to manage the little money we had. Adorned with bulbs, lights, and lots of tinsel to fill in the gaps our tree was beautiful indeed.

Chapter Twenty-Five

The Canning Jars

What good horror novel or film doesn't have a scene or two involving an underground room? It's a sure scene stealer – guaranteed to make your heart beat just a little quicker as you feel your breath catch, imagining what's just around the corner, or perhaps under the stairs. My grandmother's cellar would have provided the perfect movie location, no props necessary, to set the stage for any classic thriller. It was one of the two places in the house that filled me with trepidation; the second being the attic.

Oh, how I would dread when my mother would decide that her recipe for our evening supper required a trip down "there" to fetch an ingredient from the storage room. Access to the cellar was through a door in the hallway adjoining my grandmother's living room. Sounds like a pretty run-of-the-mill scenario; that is, until you slipped the hook-and-eye latch and pulled open the door. There was no light switch to reach for; the rooms below had no electricity. Instead, I was greeted

The Canning Jars

by pure darkness intermixed with the heavy scent of old soil as I stood momentarily locked in place at the top of the stairs. The beam of the flashlight in my hand seemed to do little to penetrate its depths, but managed to illuminate the stairs just enough to highlight the dusty cobwebs hanging perilously off the stairwell ceiling. My skin crawls even now as I recapture the memory with words. Spiders were the thing of nightmares for me; and I was about to step into their parlor – uninvited perhaps, but awaited nonetheless. Then there were those other unseen creepy-crawlies lurking underneath the open stairwell, ready to make their way up my pant leg or worse, under it.

These were not merely the musings of an over-active imagination; oh, no. Since I was very young, my brother, aptly nicknamed "The Bug," had kept a nasty assortment of insects in jars. He had, more than once, alluded to the fact that he may have *inadvertently* left a cap off a bottle or two, allowing some nasty thing with too many legs to escape. "Had I seen them anywhere?" he remarked casually, suggesting that I may well encounter them. On my way down the stairs, I'd inevitably recall the look on his face as he slyly shared a knowing wink of his eye, tormenting me.

Even so, my brother's commentary wasn't the only thing on my mind as I stood bracing myself for the descent. A chill ran down my spine as I envisioned the crypt-like stone rooms, winding from one to the next, dirt floors permeating the stagnant air with the scent of musty earth. Deep within these walls, my mother would encounter the ghost of her long-dead

Silence

father in her dreams. I never met my grandfather, Carmine, as he crossed to the other world long before I was conceived. He was kept alive through stories that echoed the joy and deep sadness of losing someone you love dearly. I knew from these poignant memories that my mother and her father shared a very special bond indeed. The two were intertwined still. My connection to him came from the present time, derived from the precognitive dreams of my mother. Innocently enough, she would always find herself deep within the catacombs of the cellar helping him shovel coal for the furnace, just as she had when she was a young girl. Connie, with her sturdy build, would always be the one to help her father stoke the massive boiler that heated the rooms above. It was time spent together that she savored. Given their relationship, one would think this innocent enough; no cause for alarm, no reason for distress. Except, I knew full well from experience that the third person in the dream, the one who would be talking in fluent Italian to my grandfather, would invariably die within a short time later. The telltale sign of one of my mother's premonitions would be the sight of her one and only black linen dress brought out of its slumber amidst the moth balls, big shiny black glass buttons gleaming as in hung ominously on the porch; "airing out" in preparation for an upcoming funeral. While my mother didn't seem to get too rattled being with the spirit of my grandfather, it wasn't something that I wanted to experience firsthand. Yet, here I was, about to enter his realm.

The Canning Jars

And so it was, with terror as my companion, I would head into the abyss in search of canned green beans. There I stood at the threshold coaxing myself to go downwards, checking my Eveready; switching it on-and-off until I was sure it was in good working order. Reaching out for the banister to steady me, my right hand hesitantly touched the old wood, careful not to grip too hard lest I pierce my hand with a sliver inflicted from the aged pine. Trapped in suspended animation, foot in midair heading for that first step, I contemplated turning back before it was too late. With a thud, I realized my foot had made contact with the stair, my fate sealed. Steadying myself and holding the flashlight rigidly in my hand, I willed my body to continue. My mind was a whirl of visions of things that go bump in the night; knowing that there was a reality that laid just beyond our consciousness that recognized them as fact. I continued downwards, counting the number of stairs aloud, the sound of my own voice little comfort. A shudder moved down my spine as something squished beneath my foot. I dared not imagine the ruined corpse. Finally, I reached the last stair. Landing on the hard-packed dirt floor, dust motes were sent scurrying like miniature tumbleweeds across the floor. Now, out in the open, the darkness felt thick and heavy. I knew the store room stood directly in front of me, albeit several feet away. Gingerly, I trudged towards my destination – shadows everywhere, enhanced by the flicker of light playing against dark. I focused on what laid ahead, ignoring the chill of the air creeping in all around me. The doorway in sight, my shaking hand reached out and gingerly made contact. Lifting the heavy

Silence

latch, then slipping my trembling fingers through the cold metal handle, I concentrated on keeping the beam of light aimed towards the entrance. Pulling the handgrip, I stepped back to accommodate its girth. With a moan capable of debilitating the bravest soul, the wooden knotty pine door swung open, its hinges lamenting the intrusion. Holding onto the frame, I pulled myself up into the waiting chamber...the spring-loaded egress closing behind me.

Flicking the light around the room, I searched the darkness. The sooty shelves that reached from floor to ceiling stood all around me as I studied them in search of tonight's missing dinner ingredient. There were countless dusty glass jars, their lids held in place with rubber rings and heavy metal latches, their eerie-looking contents held prisoner within. It's amazing how the absence of light transforms even something as simple as canned fruits and vegetables into ghastly looking things resembling something otherworldly. Somewhere between the interplay of reality and my imagination, I found the culprit responsible for bringing me here – green beans, Blue Lake beauties to be precise. As I reached up to retrieve them from the shelf, I simultaneously perceived the distinct feeling of something fuzzy crawling along my arm – the tingling of too many legs touching my skin. Instinctively, with surprising speed, I reached out to swat it away – unwilling to see exactly what it was. In that one single action I not only connected with the unknown aggressor, but dropped my only source of light onto the floor where it landed amidst God knows what else that

The Canning Jars

lurked there. The traumatic landing caused the device to fail. I found myself in a room devoid of light and sound, instantly frantic. Bending down, I swept the air close to the floor with my hand trying to connect with my salvation. It was then I thought I heard quiet, slow footfalls just outside the door. My breath stopped and my heart froze, as I strained my ears to hear. There had been no sound of anyone coming down the stairs...just the sound of feet on dirt. I stood motionless in the silence. I had no voice to call out. Fear had control of my vocal cords. Willing myself to move, my foot connected with the flashlight. Reaching down, I grasped it, my ice cold hand flipping the switch that would illuminate my prison. No light returned. I shook it wildly until the faint beam was restored and became stronger. Aiming the shaft of light towards the only exit, I stood there immobile, listening. All was silent. My mind was totally convinced something or someone was on the other side. Somehow, I could feel its presence. I desperately wanted out of this room, but terror stopped me from opening the door. Convincing myself that I had been "hearing things," I forced myself to act. Turning backwards, I snatched the green beans off the shelf. I would not leave this ordeal empty-handed. Taking the deepest breath I could muster, I swallowed hard and opened the door. Stillness invaded the space. There was nothing in the beam of light except for the staircase ahead. In a mad dash, I bolted out of the room, door slamming shut in my wake. Flying up the stairs fueled by the rush of adrenaline, I reached the top, never even connecting with the handrail. Once safely in the hallway, turning to close the door, I was

Silence

inescapably drawn to look back into the void. It was then I saw the fleeting shape of a heavy set man looking up at me - *my grandfather?* In a blink, there was nothing left – only the green beans for dinner.

Chapter Twenty-Six

The Allergy Shots

Growing up, I always remember having some general difficulty breathing. I spent a lot of time experiencing sinus headaches that almost always turned into some level of infection in my nose, or worse yet, my ears. My face would ache so much that my teeth hurt when I took even the slightest step across the floor; never mind what it felt like to blow my nose. Inevitably, my eyes would throb from the blinding light of a 60-watt bulb that felt as if I was looking directly into the midday sun. Lucky are those that have never experienced the pain of having your face feel like there was so much pressure behind its skeletal walls that you thought they might explode at any time. Even worse were the times when I practically wished it would, just to bring the pain to a standstill.

Many were the trips downtown to the office of our beloved family physician, Dr. Roger Sullivan. The trip was about a thirty-minute walk from our house. My mother's cane tapped the sidewalk with each footfall, setting the pace. Holding my

Silence

hand, she reassured me that all would be okay. It would have been nice to get there quicker, but my mother never learned how to drive a car. It was a moot point, since we wouldn't have been able to afford one anyway. We took a taxi once in a while if there was some extra cash; a "splurge," as my mother would call it. The doctor's office was located in a grand old building with two ornately carved metal doors. The address, "226 Main Street," glimmered in gold on the darkened glass panels, announcing that we had arrived at our destination. Try as I might, my skinny little arms could never pull the heavy door open. It felt as if it were locked in place. A good tug from my mother was required, followed by me holding it open with all my might so she could maneuver her rather large frame through the doorway. Once inside, the big wooden bench beckoned to my mother to sit and take it easy, as she'd be tired from the exertion of the walk. I would venture a few feet away from her, taking it all in, captivated by the sheer immensity of it all. There were towering ceilings with gigantic chandeliers that looked like they should be in an old gothic church. Their yellow light illuminated the fancy gold veins running through the shiny marble walls. The floors were made of the same marble with a beautiful runner leading to the elevator.

After a few moments, my mother would be rested. I'd try to linger as long as I could to postpone the impending elevator ride to floor number three. I was not fond of this particular mode of transportation, but since my mother had a bad back, the stairs were not an option. She'd push the big black button

The Allergy Shots

to summon the elevator. I'd stand there listening to the noisy clunking sound made by its descent to the main floor. A sudden loud thump would herald its arrival. The door would open slowly, revealing the inner gate. It creaked with an eerie moan as the gray gloved hand of the elevator operator pulled it open slowly. This was always followed by a nod from the ancient-looking old man, his pure white hair under his cap setting off deep blue eyes that seemed to look right through you. With great solemnity, he would ask what floor we wanted, standing as straight as he could muster. He would close the gate with the deliberate action of practice made perfect. Then he would start the elevator again, manually using a device that would take us to the desired floor. I'd distract myself by staring at the shiny gold buttons on his well-worn grey uniform as we jerked upwards. We would always have to wait a moment or two for him to get the floor lined up with the elevator so we could exit. At last satisfied, he would drag the gate open, the endless ride finally over. Thankfully, Dr. Sullivan's office always felt like someone's living room, homey and welcoming just like the man. If it weren't for the elevator, I wouldn't have half-minded the visit. Dr. Sullivan tried his best to get me "fixed up," as he'd call it.

My "condition" never quite seemed to away completely but rather it simply recurred on a regular basis. That's how I landed up going to see Dr. Kramer, the big-city specialist, to find out if allergies were the cause behind my constant sinus problems. Traveling to the city; namely, Hartford, was quite the trick. It

Silence

was a combination of both excitement and dread. When I was a kid, leaving New Britain to go to Hartford was a big deal. It was quite the destination. Macy's department store on Main Street with its huge front windows beckoned enthralled passersby to come into its magical world. Trips here were infrequent, mainly because it took two buses and enough money to make it for special occasions only. And a special occasion it would have been if it weren't for the fact that I was going to see an allergy specialist. I had no idea of what to expect, and my mother no doubt underplayed it to give me the best sense of security she could offer.

Dr. Kramer's office was located on Trumbull Street on the tenth floor. At least big city elevators didn't creak, thank God. But as we stood solemnly in the sterile chamber, I genuinely missed the old man in the gray uniform; the ride was cold and impersonal. This feeling continued as we entered the doctor's office. Gone was the comforting feeling that welcomed me at Dr. Sullivan's. Instead, at Dr. Kramer's, we were greeted by stark white walls, black chairs lined up against them like soldiers. My discomfort escalated when I realized there were floor to ceiling windows opposite the seating area; further confirmation we were in a skyscraper not a cozy old building. This put the icing on the cake for me, my fear level now turned up to high. While the waiting room chairs weren't all that close to the windows, my acrophobia kept me feeling as though I had to sit firmly planted in my chair to keep from being sucked right out the window. When my name was called, I wrenched

The Allergy Shots

myself out of my seat; legs stiff from tension, I walked across the room like an arthritic old woman. Inching my body towards the receptionist's desk with my eyes riveted to the floor, I kept a "safe" distance from the dreaded windows I was sure would lead to my early demise should I stray too close. We followed the nurse in her crisp white uniform and cap down the hall in silence, not a word uttered aloud until we reached the door to the office. The nurse stopped abruptly, the rubber soles of her impeccably clean white shoes causing her body to jerk forward slightly as she did so. With a knowing look, she instructed us to take a seat inside to await our "consultation" with the doctor. My mother and I sat side-by-side in the huge black leather chairs facing the gleaming silver and glass desk that belonged to Dr. Kramer. My trepidation continued to build. I felt like a tiny speck on the huge chair my feet dangling in midair. By the time the doctor made his appearance, my fear level was through the roof. Dr. Kramer walked in looking like a very elegant Boris Karloff, dressed impeccably in a crisp white jacket devoid of the smallest wrinkle. I remembering fixating on the small black block letters, embroidered just mid chest level on the left side of his jacket, spelling out his name in upper and lower case. I don't recall much more of what was said, but do remember feeling fairly petrified; my mother's reassurances not quite penetrating my fear.

The doctor left his office saying something about meeting us in the treatment room in a few moments. Another nurse came in shortly afterwards and escorted by mother and I down another

Silence

long corridor into a stark white room stainless steel countertops gleaming. I remember the feel of the stool under my feet as I climbed up to sit on the examination table, its crisp white paper crunching beneath me. I couldn't help catching sight of the two stainless steel cases nearby, their covers concealing their contents from view. This struck me as ominous and the look on my mother's face mirrored my feelings, her slight smile trying to console me. My fears certainly were confirmed when Dr. Kramer walked in and positioned himself on my right while his nurse, in response to a slight nod in her direction from the doctor, expertly flipped open one of the covers revealing an endless row of hypodermic needles neatly arranged in their own individual slots. I momentarily looked away to banish the sight. The doctor was talking to my mother. I didn't comprehend what they were saying, as I felt the cold wet alcohol slide down my arm. Wide open, my eyes followed the nurse's deft fingers as, pen in hand, she began to write a series of numbers down my arm in two columns ending with the number 20. As she handed the first hypodermic to the doctor's waiting hand, I felt myself disappear.

Chapter Twenty-Seven

Grant Hill Clinic

My journey into the nightmarish world of allergy shots was to continue for the next several years as it had been discovered that an allergy to mold was why I had so much difficulty breathing. My mother faced a very difficult predicament with this diagnosis because we had very limited funds and the cost of bi-weekly excursions to Hartford for continuing treatment was impossible. And so it was that we were referred to the office of Dr. Raleigh, an ear-nose-throat specialist who agreed to take me on as a patient. I would make the lengthy trek to his office on foot and alone; my mother's back kept her from accompanying me except for our very first visit to meet Dr. Raleigh when we indulged on a taxi since it wasn't on a bus route. Every two weeks after school, I would report to the doctor's office like clockwork. If I was lucky enough, I'd get a seat inside his small waiting room. There was something slightly comforting about the place, dimly lit as it was by small lamps on tables strategically placed between every few chairs – the kind that were covered in imitation

Silence

leather. They would always squish a bit when you sat in them, obviously having seen better days. On days when there were lots of patients, I'd land up sitting out in the hallway on some folding chairs relegated to overflow usually by myself. I hated sitting there because people passing by would always give you a strange look, wondering what was wrong with you. I felt uncomfortable in my seat, the imploring looks wondering why I wasn't sitting there with an adult at the tender age of twelve. I became adept at dropping into that space inside me where sound became quiet and the comments went unheard.

I'd be rescued by Dr. Raleigh's nurse, Mrs. Ross, who I remember to this day for her kindness and gentle spirit; she was my lifesaver. A mere sprite of a woman, her white hair always neat and short, tortoise shell glasses framing her face, she'd always escort me with a supportive arm around my shoulders into the small room where I'd get my shots. Her clear blue eyes spoke volumes to me; she understood from the heart that I was just a kid, scared of needles yet forced to get them regularly to keep my allergies in check. Mrs. Ross could put me at ease in an instant, and I'd hardly notice the two shots, one in each arm as she engaged me in conversation about school or something else to distract me. She made all the difference in the world.

The toughest part of these visits always came when I would go up to the desk to make my next appointment and pay the receptionist. I'll never forget the way she looked. She had the most beautiful pale white skin, her shoulder length blonde hair worn in the classic side-parted pageboy style. She would toss

Grant Hill Clinic

her head gently back like a movie star as she looked up from her paperwork, her hair swinging in slow motion just like the woman in the Prell shampoo commercial. I'd be drawn out of my reverie as she spoke, remembering to take out the four one-dollar bills to put "on account" for my visit. Madeline would do the best she could to keep from having her clear blue eyes turn misty when she had to remind me to tell my mother that I'd need to bring more money to catch up on the "arrears," as she would call it. This was always mortifying to me because her desk sat right in front of everyone in the small waiting room. It was right out in the open where everyone could hear even the quietest of comments. When I would turn away from the desk, people would avert their eyes, pretending to be reading their magazines, while others would shake their heads as if they couldn't understand how someone couldn't pay their bills. Some of the kinder ones would smile at me, trying to put the *kid in the spotlight* at ease. They could never understand my embarrassment but could clearly see my telltale reddening face. I'd always feel like I was shrinking inside as I walked out of the office, trying to disappear yet unable to do so because my throbbing arms would bring me back to reality.

As I left the building and started walking back towards home, I would get myself ready for the next phase of the trip. Never a brave kid, I always felt very vulnerable because of my size. I was all skin and bones, with my hand-me-downs adding to the effect. Exceedingly shy from being tormented by my brother, self-confidence was not something that kept

Silence

me company, ever. In order to get home before it got dark – something I definitely wanted to avoid – I'd have to take a short cut on a street that was bordered by two huge factory buildings, one on each side. The mammoths loomed high above the road, their solid brick facades creating the feeling of being caught inside a tunnel with no easy escape. The noise emanating from the machinery running tirelessly within their walls was so loud that as I passed between them, I couldn't even hear my own voice as I spoke out loud in an attempt to reassure myself that everything would be fine. The niggling thought that no one would ever hear me if something happened to me always made my heart pound. I had a ritual I would perform to brace myself for the trek. Before entering into the "tunnel," as I nicknamed it, I would pick up the large rock that I had left hidden under the bush on the corner of the street. As I clutched it in my hand with my arm at my side, I felt stronger. Somehow knowing that I had this rock and could throw it at anyone that might try to harm me gave me a small sense of security. Thinking back on this now, I see the scared child I was, and I am glad that I believed that myth. Chances are it would have done little or nothing in defense, given my notably bad aim when attempting to throw even a snowball. On most days, I'd make it through fine, letting my over-active imagination relax as I neared the end of the passageway. A few steps further and I was out in the open, leaving my beloved protector – the rock – under another bush at the end of the street where it would wait secretly until next time.

Grant Hill Clinic

One day in late October, I began my shortcut commencing with my usual ritual. I had been doing well building up my courage for "the tunnel" and felt pretty good because, outside of the scenarios created in the mind of a scared child, things had been safe. Halfway down the road, I decided that I should put down my trusty friend the rock and give myself a break from its weight. I continued walking, feeling much braver than I ever had, when I had that eerily distinct feeling that you get when you know that you've just made a mistake. Out of the corner of my eye I saw the big black car approaching. I tried valiantly to make myself believe that it was not slowing down and pulling over. I walked closer to the building and began to walk faster. The body of the car kept pace with me; then, quickly moved ahead. I sighed heavily and let out the breath I had been holding on to for dear life. Suddenly, the car pulled over the curb and the passenger door swung open blocking part of the sidewalk in front of me. The man inside the darkened interior leaned towards the opening. I froze, no rock – no protection. *In a syrupy sweet voice, he asked me if I wanted a ride. He'd be happy to take me home – just hop inside.* I tried to answer him, but no words would come. My fear was coming alive right in front of me; as he continued to lure me inwards. Out of nowhere, a scream pierced the air – one so primal that it took a moment for me to realize it was my own voice. Something inside of me took hold and I turned and ran in the opposite direction as fast as I could. I collided with a factory worker who had come out through an unseen door in

Silence

the building – inadvertently becoming my savior. The door of the black sedan slammed shut and the car sped off.

The next time I went to the doctor's office, I knew I wouldn't be taking the shortcut again. It proved to be my last trip, anyway. When I walked into the office and up to Madeline's desk to check in, she told me to wait a moment rather than take a seat to await my turn to be seen. She came back and handed me a box she said contained my allergy medicine. I didn't immediately understand what she said next – the voice I heard felt uncharacteristically cold and devoid of feeling. When I asked her to repeat herself, I heard her loud and clear as did everyone else in earshot. She advised me that I should let my mother know that because we could not pay our account in full, it was necessary for us to find another doctor. I stood there powerless, clutching the box in my hand, as hot tears began to roll down my face. It was then that my beloved Mrs. Ross appeared from nowhere. Without a word, she placed her arm around my shoulder gently and led me to the familiar examination room. Her kindhearted eyes spoke volumes as she dried my tears. Taking the box from my hand, she gave me my allergy shots for the last time.

Chapter Twenty-Eight

The Empty Bra Cup

I sit here yearning to get back into writing and yet finding myself wandering – emotionally, mentally and physically. I leave my desk to make some toast. It immediately satisfies some inner craving for comfort. *Is it the cold snowy day or something more?* Next, I take the time to pay a few bills, telling myself that getting the request for payment processed early is the efficient thing to do. Somewhere this registers as a distraction. Still, without missing a beat, I find myself online ordering a new cookbook – as if I truly need another. Finally, I begin to settle in to review what I had written so far. Two paragraphs later, I'm abruptly interrupted with the thought that I should go and check to see if the mailman had arrived. Before jumping out of my chair to do so, I ask myself: *What the heck am I doing?* The answer materialized with all the clarity of a gigantic neon billboard: *You are distracting yourself!* I will admit to having a habit of doing this, something my husband, Kurt, will no doubt love to see me put in writing. Apparently, I am quite good at this type of thing. I think about how I learned

Silence

to practice the fine art of diversion to avoid hurting someone's feelings or to protect them from an outside source of sorrow. *The truth is that I am about to embark on one of those connect-the-dot moments from my childhood*

The question before me is: *Why the distractions – one right after another?* The answer is fairly simple. I decided that I would write this book without outlines – just let it happen – see what came up for me. Today, it's all about the realization that I take myself out of situations that feel uncomfortable. Apparently, I've had lots of practice. I just never realized that it's more than just a habit, it's a protective mechanism. Letting my guard down, there are lots of memories starting to flood my mind. One, in particular, jumps into my recollection without a moment's hesitation. It involves the caustic comments of a thirteen-year-old boy whose name I've never forgotten to this day.

Suddenly, Deborah – the strong woman, seems to have been instantly replaced by Debbie, the weak and skinny kid with the empty training bra – the "one-size fits all" stretchy thing my sister bought me at D & L's department store in an effort to make me feel better about being flat-chested. I'm in a classroom minding my own business, working on my assignment just like the teacher told us to do before she had to step out of the classroom for a few minutes. Unlike me, a kid named Reed thought it better use of his time to single me out to be the butt of his latest barrage of mean commentary, featuring crude remarks about my lack of breasts. I sat transfixed at my

The Empty Bra Cup

desk, trying to pretend that I didn't hear his comments nor the laughter of what felt like everyone in the room as it rose with the intensity of a tsunami. My body was betraying my façade, as I felt the heat rising in my face which was, no doubt, turning a brilliant shade of red. Determined to barricade myself from the onslaught, I buried myself deeper into the textbook on the desk before me. I watched as the color drained from my hands. Frozen in my chair, my body betrayed me as I began to tremble, slightly at first...an almost imperceptible movement. In a sudden explosion, my entire body was visibly quaking, the roar in my ears deafening. This, of course, only added fuel to the fire. From deep within, I felt a heaviness begin to encompass me in a quiet fog. The laughing children became eerily quiet; the scene had become a silent movie with me in the starring role.

Chapter Twenty-Nine

The Volleyball Net

Dentistry never played a very big part in growing up for me; I can't recall ever seeing a "real" dentist until age twenty when I was married. Sure, I brushed my teeth regularly; my mother had taught me the basics of good oral hygiene. It's just that in our family, unless you got really sick or you had a bad toothache, you didn't go to the doctor. Money was scarce; looking back from my current vantage point, I realize my mother could stretch a dollar further than any human being I know. Dentists, however, didn't make the cut. We never had soda in our house, or for that matter, not many sugary treats either, so my teeth held up pretty well. My baby teeth stayed intact for an amazingly long time. I have distinct memories of my mother removing a few of them for me when they became seriously loose. However, she never had the stomach to just pull one out, even if it was dangling. Instead, the procedure was to sit on the closed toilet bowl seat and brace myself, gingerly opening my mouth as wide as I could, while I waited with trepidation for the process to begin. My mother's method of

The Volleyball Net

tooth removal was to slip a loop of heavy quilting thread around the base of the tooth, leaving a long piece of thread which she expertly wrapped around her finger. Her hand would close tightly, and on the count of three, a strong yank on the thread jettisoned the culprit from its stronghold. Sometimes, it didn't work on the first try – you can imagine that scenario without any words. Salt and water gargle followed by biting down on a wet teabag and *voila*, the ordeal was over. At least physically. Who needed a dentist? Once, my brother decided he wanted to give it a go and experimented with a small pillow and a punch to my jaw. This invariably made the first option a clear choice in my mind.

As far as tooth decay prevention was concerned, I got the fluoride "treatments" offered at elementary school. When the teacher would hand out the forms requiring a parent's signature to authorize the treatment, I dreaded handing it to my mother. For a brief moment or two, I'd think about losing the paperwork, but my early inability to challenge authority in any way always kept me from doing so. Soon enough, the day would come for "the treatment." We'd wait for the announcement over the loud speaker in our classroom that alerted our teacher that it was our class's turn. She would obligingly march us single-file down to the makeshift space in the corner of the gymnasium set aside for this sole purpose. Rows of chairs, the kind with the wooden writing surface attached, stood lined up one after the other, waiting silently for their victims to be seated. Like a row of dominoes falling in sync, we'd open our mouths wide

Silence

for the archaic metal apparatus that could best be described as a holder for a tampon-like object which had been soaked with some concoction containing fluoride. It was placed into the side of your mouth, a small part of it dangling precariously over your bottom lip. Once positioned, the nurse would instruct you to close your mouth, as she clamped the device under your chin thereby effectively securing the evil contraption in place. The torture would last five minutes but it seemed like hours. It would always cause me to gag almost instantly, tears streaming down my face from trying to stop the reflex. When I would raise my hand to draw attention from the nurse, her practiced response was to tell you to relax and let the fluoride do its job. Her words brought no amount of comfort, and she appeared impervious to what was unfolding in front of her. Nevertheless, it was becoming impossible for me to hold back the sensation of choking. The agonizing minutes dragged by like an eternity as I silently prayed for it to be over. I'd find myself shaking by the time the nurse would release the tortuous device and tell us to "spit". We would have to wait another thirty minutes in the chair to guarantee that we would not eat or drink during that time period. All the while, a taste as vile as one could imagine permeated your mouth; something akin to a mouthful of nasty rusted metal.

I would learn from a dentist years later that I, indeed, have a very small space inside my mouth. To this day, I have great difficulty having x-rays taken. This explains why it never appeared to trouble the other children as much as it did me. It

The Volleyball Net

gave them plenty of fodder for their cruel jokes during recess, grabbing their throats and pretending to choke as they laughed at me. I'd do what I could to pretend I wasn't listening, always retreating silently into myself as I disappeared like a cloud evaporating in the sky. A perpetual state of apprehension became a mainstay for me as far as my teeth were concerned. The thing that really changed me and exaggerated my shyness was that when my adult teeth grew in, the two canines were missing. This apparently was a hereditary deficit as my mother bore the same trademark until she opted for dentures later in life. You'll see very few smiling pictures of my mother when she was young; obviously, she bore the embarrassment of missing teeth in a manner similar to myself. I'd always attempt to smile as little as possible but never enough to escape being teased about having picket-fence teeth. For some reason, it appeared that I would grow up producing enough fodder to be the brunt of others' jokes throughout my school years.

The worst instance of all occurred in eighth grade, I was the ripe old age of thirteen. One fateful day, I was scheduled for fourth-period gym class. To say I disliked gym was a gross understatement. It all started with having to change into our gym outfit which consisted of a one-piece navy blue contraption that had short pant legs. The experience of having to change clothes in front of other girls who had begun to blossom into womanhood while I remained in what felt like an eternal child-like body felt degrading. My stretch bra was worn mainly to replace an undershirt but for little else. This never went without

Silence

notice, as I was always the "odd one out," and several of the more endowed girls never missed an opportunity to make a caustic comment here or there. This resulted outwardly in a reddened face but inwardly in silent tears. I'd learned to keep them hidden as a matter of survival.

Little did I know; the worst was yet to come as it was volleyball day. There was never a person born that sucked at playing volleyball more than me, and everyone in school knew it. When it came to choosing teams, I never got picked. I was always "assigned" by the gym teacher to one instead, amidst moans and groans from the unlucky girls that I would play with. To say I felt alienated just didn't cover the scope of my feelings. This one particular day, the gym teacher chose to rotate the players from back to front instead of letting us choose our choice of positions. I generally would stay as far back and out of the way as possible. This way everyone else could literally run back and forth without me being in the way. The other team would always try to hit the ball squarely towards me, knowing that the odds were I'd miss it. At least this way, my team stood a chance; I liked to think my fellow teammates – I use that term loosely – actually appreciated my thoughtfulness. As the rotation continued, I inevitably found myself in a front line position. Sweat covered my face, not from the physical activity of the game, but from the sheer fear of standing face-to-face with someone glaring at me from across the net. Everyone on my team dreaded this moment, whilst the other side had been eagerly awaiting it. The game was on, the ball was served in

The Volleyball Net

my direction, one of the girls darted in front of me to hit the ball back across the net, and I was saved from folly for a brief moment. Then, suddenly, the ball was right in front of me with no space for someone to intercede. Hearing pleading screams of "hit it over, hit it over," I made a grand attempt to connect my hands with the ball. As I ran towards the net, something happened that to this day defies explanation. In the split second that I jumped up to hit the ball, my face simultaneously hit the net. Instead of bouncing back, my front teeth connected with the fabric of the net and ensnared me. I tried to pull back, to no avail, as my picket fence teeth clearly had other plans. I was a fish caught in a net unable to free myself. Within seconds, everyone recognized what had happened. The faces of the girls appeared in front of my eyes in slow motion as their laughter rose from the floor and resounded throughout the gym, ruthlessly echoing off the walls. I struggled hopelessly with the net, but I couldn't get untangled. My eyes pleaded for mercy as I searched for the gym teacher. Why wasn't she helping me, where was she? I connected with her through the corner of my eye and caught her laughing along with the rest of them – except she managed to have the discretion to cover her mouth. In what felt like eons to me, she finally came over to the net and removed it from my mouth. No longer hooked like a whimpering fish pleading to be released, I did the only thing that came to me. Without a second's hesitation, I turned and ran to the dressing room, grabbed my clothes and books and fled the building. I didn't look back for an instant and no one tried to stop me. The news of this "memorable" event spread like

Silence

wildfire throughout the school. I bore the embarrassment of this moment for what seemed like forever. My mother wrote me a note that got me out of gym class for the rest of the remaining two months of school. No one missed me in that class; I'm certain of that. Instead, I spent my time in study hall, a place where I could bury myself in my beloved books without the need to communicate with anyone. For at least one period a day, I was free.

Chapter Thirty

The White Horse

My brother had a strange cavalcade of friends. When I think about it, I have to use the term "friends" loosely, they were more like acquaintances. They were always in the periphery of things whenever they were at our house, moving shadow-like and always appearing like a blur between edginess and the inert blankness of a zombie. Being as naïve as I was, it took a while for me to catch on to the fact that their appearance solely depended on whether they had "used" or not. This was a word that I picked up from a distance, hearing my brother talking from the other room. While I never quite understood exactly what that meant at the time, I knew it wasn't something I cared to know anything about either. His cohorts always mulled about in the kitchen upon arriving; finally, settling down at the table leaning in towards the center like accomplices talking over their latest plot. Most memorable was John, the guy who always dressed impeccably in those strange iridescent gray "shark-skin" suits, his starched black shirt formally buttoned to the neck albeit with the absence of a

Silence

tie. Shiny black pointy-tip boots flashed out from beneath the crisp front pleat of his pants, and never looked scuffed or worn. His hair had the tight wiriness of my brother's. I imagined him going through the daily ritual of getting every unruly hair in place, brushed back like Dracula complete with widow's peak, the slickness replaced instead with layers of Aqua Net hairspray. The smallest tuft of hair was poised in the cleft of his chin while the rest of his face remained clean shaven. I'll always remember his hands; in particular, his fingernails which were perfectly manicured and short – not a trace of dirt resided there. His gold ring with square black onyx would flash as he habitually played with the tiny goatee, the long nail on his pinky finger strikingly different than the rest.

Cohort number two, Jerry, was a complete visual opposite of John. Clad in dingy khaki army jacket and worn out looking jeans, he always sported a baggy faded tee shirt to complete his ensemble. Keep in mind, this was not the "in" style of the day, so he was not in any way making a fashion statement. Always keeping his head down, his stringy dark hair swung across his face like a mop going across a floor. While John sauntered in with the air of a Kentucky gentleman, Jerry's stride echoed with the "clomp" of army boots. If they happened to be at our house at the same time, John always kept his distance, not willing to risk coming into physical contact with his clothing and Jerry.

My brother echoed the cleanliness of John but in a much more understated way. He didn't stand out in his Banlon smooth

The White Horse

knit polo shirt and ironed jeans which is exactly the way he wanted it. Cool doesn't require flash, if you catch my drift.

Visits by these two were usually intermittent and didn't last long. The exception was the time I came home from school early and walked in on a trail of water and ice cubes across the linoleum floor of our living room. There was an uneasiness in the air as I closed the door behind me, noticing that the door to the hallway was latched, something very unusual. I knew my mother wasn't home as there was no way this disarray would exist. I had noticed Jerry's old beater of a car out front but didn't see him or my brother immediately. Only after I followed the intermittent puddles did I hear muffled sounds coming from the bathroom. I stood transfixed in the middle of the kitchen staring blankly, sensing danger but as frozen in place as ice in a tray. The sound of my brother's frenzied voice came from inside, as I watched water ooze silently from under the wooden frame of the entry. Suddenly, the door jerked open. Startled momentarily, Junior. stood there fully clothed and soaking wet. From behind him I glimpsed the tub in the tiny room, partially covered by the open door. Jerry's head was leaning back against the wall, his face milky white and drawn. His body was submerged in what looked like a tub of ice. Just behind my brother's feet lay Jerry's familiar khaki jacket, now a soggy pile of cloth. In response to the horror unfolding before me, I felt myself begin to shake, tremors coming from deep within. Junior's voice sounded muffled as he shouted for me to go outside. As he came closer to me, my muscles woke up and

Silence

made my legs move obligingly away from the ghastly sight. The hypodermic needle laying on the kitchen table disappeared like an illusion in my brother's hands, as I made my way past.

For what seemed like an eternity, I sat on the back porch in without making a single sound. I was too petrified to do anything more, after my brother "cautioned" me not to move until he came out again. Thoughts raced through my head, I was sure Jerry was dead. Although he came as close to a near death experience as he could, Jerry survived what I later learned was a near overdose. His "ride on the white horse" had been nearly fatal. Nothing was ever said of the event, the remains cleaned up as if it never occurred. My brother's cronies disappeared for a while, no doubt the result of my mother's hand in the matter, quietly shrouding the aftermath with good old-fashioned silence.

Experiencing Jerry's near demise as a naive thirteen-year-old was horrific; yet, it didn't prepare me for what was about to transpire later that same year. Things had quieted down considerably following the "incident" until one run-of-the-mill Saturday afternoon. My mother was out-and-about visiting some of our more elderly neighbors, just "checking in," as was her custom. Connie, as the neighbors called her, would make the rounds bringing fresh-baked cookies or muffins along with her to share with a cup of tea, spending time with people who some had forgotten. The old women would repeat their stories while my mother listened intently, as if it were the first time

The White Horse

being told. I'm certain her visits were the highlight of many of their days.

This particular afternoon I preferred to curl up, blanketed on the couch with a good book to pass the time. A few oatmeal walnut cookies fresh out of the oven, a glass of milk, and my beloved cat keeping me company made an idyllic picture. And so it was that my mom went on her way and I settled in to read. Immersed in the tales and poems of Edgar Allan Poe, a favorite of both mine and my mother's, the afternoon was peaceful and quiet. My brother came home as I delved into *The Cask of Amontillado*, startling me as he entered through the back door. He didn't say much of anything as he breezed by heading upstairs to his room. I went back to reading as raindrops started to fall on the windowpane, adding the perfect backdrop to my book. Engrossed in my favorite pastime I was once again swept away to another time and place – until I heard the undeniable thud overhead. Startled by the heaviness of the sound, as it seemed to vibrate the ceiling above me, I was brought back instantly to the confines of our living room. I waited to hear what would come next, but there was only the echo of silence. Something felt wrong as I moved across the room to the hallway door. Seeking an answer for the mysterious thud, I shouted upstairs to my brother. There was no reply; the hair on the back of my neck began to tingle. I knew it wasn't just the novel I was reading, as the sense of impending doom spread down the stairwell engulfing me. Drawn up the stairs by that curious attraction that enfolds us in these kinds of circumstances, I

Silence

took one step at a time, holding onto the banister to steady me as I moved upwards. My least favorite place in the house – the attic – was right in the middle of the two rooms upstairs. That fact alone evoked anxiety enough, never mind what might lie ahead. I reached the top stair and landing – calling out once again to my brother through his closed bedroom door. It was as quiet as a graveyard, not a sound to be heard. Instinctively, I knew I had to open the door – something was wrong. Haltingly, I turned the old black knob and the door creaked open slowly revealing the cause of the thud. My brother lay prone on the floor. I swallowed hard, my throat seized up at the sight of his immobile body. He made no sound as I approached him, stopping on a dime when I saw the needle hanging out of his arm just below the dark yellow tourniquet. On the table beside him were the trappings responsible for his current status. Too petrified to touch him, I repeatedly called his name. Left-brain taking over, I thought logically. *I have to get help right away.* My aunt was the only choice. Her apartment was on the far side of the house we shared with my grandmother. She was usually home cleaning on Saturday. Hearing the sound of the vacuum cleaner inside, I pounded on her door. Miraculously she heard me and, upon seeing my face, followed me instantly as I explained what happened. My aunt was what we would call "the nervous type". I had wished with all my heart that she didn't need to be the one drawn into this. Climbing the stairs two at a time she went through the door as I followed. I watched the color drain out of her in the blink of an eye when she saw Junior. Her shrill scream pierced the air, the likes of which

The White Horse

I had never heard. So intense was the sound, that it brought the "corpse" on the floor back to life in an instant, scaring both of us even further as his eyes glared open and his head snapped off the floor. As we stood side-by-side transfixed in time, Junior's body began to re-animate itself. Amazingly, the first thing my brother did was yell at the both of us – accusing us of intruding on his privacy! My aunt shouted back some obscenities in Italian. Acting on auto-pilot as I was still in shock, I gave him a punch in his "good" arm for being such an ass. Unbelievably, within a short time afterward, this too passed quietly into history as if nothing had actually happened. Just another page in the story of my brother's life…and mine.

Chapter Thirty-One

The Camp Counselor Fiasco

The summer I turned fifteen I cautiously decided to step out of my comfort zone and volunteer as a camp counselor trainee at a neighborhood children's home which, at the time, was still referred to as an orphanage. I'll never forget my first assignment. Being a non-swimmer, I was mortified when the powers that be assigned me to go on an outing to a local watering hole with a group of feisty thirteen-year-old boys. Never feeling very comfortable in a bathing suit, I had a modest one-piece thing I'd drag out on rare occasions. I tried it on the morning of the field trip. As I gazed at my reflection in the mirror, I was instantly reminded of my non-endowment issue. Having been repeatedly teased about wearing training bras, I made the fateful decision to stuff the top of my suit with cotton balls. Not enough to give me the Marilyn Monroe look that would be obvious – but ample enough to make me look like the average fifteen-year-old female counselor – in order to garner the kids' respect. Memories of being teased mercilessly by other boys when I was thirteen sealed the deal. I finished

The Camp Counselor Fiasco

dressing and headed out the door. Supposing the counselor thing was mainly a high-brow babysitter job, I wasn't actually planning to swim; the most I would have to do was to get my feet wet. I knew the lifeguards on duty could take care of any risky encounters that the kids might get into in the water.

What happened next isn't that hard to figure out; especially, if as a young girl blossoming into what was perceived as a less-than-perfect body, you may have chosen some fiberfill augmentation yourself. At first, the afternoon was progressing according to plan. The kids were just glad to get outdoors and cool themselves off during the summer heat wave. The more experienced counselors, clad in bathing suits themselves, were enjoying the water while I stayed safely onshore tasked with watching everyone's belongings. This afforded me the perfect excuse to cover up my fear of water and inability to swim a single stroke, while keeping my cotton balls intact. Out of the blue, a couple of the boys decided that it would be fun to see what the new counselor was made of by testing the limits of what I would let them get away with. They grabbed my clothes from the blanket and starting running towards the water, kicking up clouds of sand. Out into the depths of the watering hole they fled, taunting me to stop them as they dangled my only dry clothes just a few feet from the surface. Running to the edge of the water I took a deep breath and, with as much self-confidence as I could muster, demanded they stop what they were doing immediately. This was about as effective as a lamb asking a pack of lions to reconsider its choice of dinner when they are

Silence

the main course. In a bold move, I assertively stepped into the water up to my ankles. In response to my action, I helplessly watched as my shorts, shirt and undergarments hit the water in seemingly slow motion. The time for any negotiation was over. I knew I had to act fast before my clothing disappeared entirely under the surface. In a momentary act of fearlessness born out of desperation, I strode out into the water. Without thought I submerged myself enough to save my clothing. The maniacal laughter of thirteen-year-old boys resonated endlessly all around me. It confirmed my inability to govern them as a counselor. Now, I'd never be taken seriously.

Just as quickly as it all happened, the kids appeared bored with their victory. Suddenly, I realized that in my daring rescue of my clothing, I had saturated my entire swimsuit. It took about thirty seconds for the boys to recognize those strange looking things floating on the water's surface; and, less time to visually follow the trail back to one red-faced counselor – me! There I was, immobile, telltale fragments of my pseudo-breasts lingering over the top of my swimsuit. There are no words to aptly describe what happened next. All eyes were suddenly turned my way as I became the afternoon's amusement. I was literally drowning with embarrassment. I couldn't even muster the strength to pretend it didn't bother me – some things defy the ability to act as if nothing has happened. There was too much evidence to the contrary, anyway. It seemed like an eternity to get from the water to the beach. Wrapping myself in a blanket, I sat doggedly alone. Not a single comrade attempted to put

The Camp Counselor Fiasco

me out of my misery. Every minute thereafter filled me with the knowledge that I would have to remain with the group for the rest of the afternoon, unable to escape. The only thing to look forward to was the dreaded bus ride back confined with my tormentors. The moment we returned, I resigned; knowing I would never be able to face these kids again and garner any kind of respect. My summer career was over before it had even begun.

Being embarrassed and self-conscious about my physical body continued to plague me throughout much of my young life. I have no doubt the many caustic encounters I endured fostered the unconscious inclination that allowed me, as I grew older, to take on so much extra body weight that it resulted in quite an ample bosom indeed.

Chapter Thirty-Two

Friendship Betrayed

Saying I exhibited shyness growing up is an understatement. Being pretty introverted, even the term wallflower wouldn't do me justice. So, how I became friends with the beautiful, sought after, extroverted Diana in the summer of tenth grade was a mystery to me. Nevertheless, we became great friends at a rapid pace. It was somehow very easy for me to talk with her about pretty much anything, and she was always interested. I was captivated by her self-confidence. I had found the girlfriend I could emulate. I could be the extrovert my soul longed to be, comfortable in her company. She had a way of putting me at ease. and I trusted her without reservation. Diana became the bona fide girlfriend that I never had. I'd spend weekends sleeping over at her house, sharing stories and dreams over hot chocolate. Over time, the answer to the mystery of our friendship became more apparent when I noticed was that I was pretty much her only girlfriend.

Friendship Betrayed

Once I got to know her better, the answer was fairly easy to figure out. Anyone who knew Diana realized she had a penchant for creating a lot of attention around herself. Not that it took much effort on her part. Virtually every guy who saw her stopped dead in his tracks as she languidly passed by. If he was lucky, she'd turn her huge, brown doe eyes in his direction and give him a wink with those lashes that even the best Maybelline mascara couldn't improve upon; it would melt them every time. To say she was a tease was probably as much an understatement as to say I was a wallflower. Most girls were busy protecting their boyfriends from Diana, although she really wasn't interested in any of them.

Since I had yet to ever have a boyfriend, I was the perfect comrade for Diana. Nevertheless, this fact didn't mean I hadn't had my share of heavy-duty, albeit one-sided, crushes. The one that specifically comes to mind was an orderly at the local hospital where Diana and I volunteered after school. We were assigned to "Mercury Service," which consisted of running errands around the hospital as needed. We reported to a few up-and-coming medical students who were currently holding the even less illustrious job of being orderlies. Mike, tall and muscular, made my heart beat wildly whenever I was in his presence. I'd be thrilled when he was on duty, occasionally catching a glimpse of the god in blue scrubs. Everything about him was perfection. His sandy blonde hair, those blue eyes that sparkled like clear gemstones. I could go on and on. I'd just about melt in my tracks when he would talk to me, even if it

Silence

was just to give me the assignment of making a pickup from the blood bank to bring to a patient floor. The only thing that mattered was that Mike was talking to me. I had it bad. I would spend hours talking with Diana about Mr. Perfect. Being the great friend she was, she listened fervently as I blathered on and on about how wonderful I thought he was. I never anticipated anything would come of it, but a girl could dream.

One day, we were in the Mercury Service office with a few other volunteers, but none of the guys were there. We were all just talking about stuff in general, when Diana began to steer the conversation in a different direction. She brought up the topic of guys; in particular, the orderlies that ran our department. One by one she was making comments about them, engaging all the other the girls in rating them. I made a few inconsequential comments just to feel like a part of the conversation. When she mentioned Mike, the comments were innocent enough. I managed to fade into the background, preferring to keep my fantasies about Mike private. Then, she began to intensify the commentary, going on and on about his looks, his body and how strong he was, and how it would feel to be in his arms – all in vivid detail. All the while, Diana was looking directly at me. I tried to avoid eye contact with her, but it was becoming increasingly more difficult with every slow-moving moment. I knew she could feel how uncomfortable I was; it wouldn't have taken a rocket scientist, much less a girl's best friend to figure it out.

Friendship Betrayed

A split second later, I felt the guillotine come crashing down on my neck. Diana came right out and said she knew someone in the room who had a big crush on Mike. I felt my face get red hot in an instant which made it obvious to everyone who she was talking about. While I sat in frozen disbelief, she started outright teasing me about it, revealing things that I had said about him in private moments between us. I was stunned. I couldn't believe that she was spilling her guts about my secrets. This was no joke, and I told her so. I pleaded with her to stop, but she seemed oblivious. Everyone's rapt attention was on me. I tried to deny my feelings, but I was hardly convincing. I found myself relenting to her barrage, and admitted my feelings towards Mike, hoping to finally get her to stop. The last syllable of "I love Mike" had barely escaped my lips, when Diana suddenly reached out and closed the door in the corner of the room. Behind it stood Mike! I stood frozen facing him, unable to move or breathe; staring into his blue eyes for what seemed an endless eternity. Somewhere in my consciousness, I knew I had to get away, but everything seemed to begin to move in slow motion. Turning away from Mike, I saw Diana standing there, smiling. All sound seemed to have become muffled, indistinguishable to me as I realized I was running out of the room and down the hallway. I found the girls' room and, once inside, barricaded the door with the garbage can. I fortified my stronghold by leaning my 110-pound frame against it for all it was worth. As I did, I felt the life force draining out of me. I'm surprised I didn't pass out. Life as I knew it moments before had ended. My heart had been torn out and served up to Mike

Silence

on a silver platter as I was simultaneously betrayed by the one person in the world I believed was my true friend.

I felt my body literally slide down the door as I gave in to the onslaught of sadness that weighed heavily inside me. Somewhere in time, I felt the door move slightly as Mike's muffled voice reached my consciousness. I couldn't distinguish exactly what he was saying, nor did I want to. *I never wanted to see him again, so how could I possibly face him?* He stayed there quietly for what seemed like an eternity. I knew he was there. I could feel him in the spaces between the silence. Again, he spoke to me, apologizing for what had happened. This time I could hear the pain in his voice when he said he had no idea what Diana had planned when he stepped behind the door. There had been no good exit point for him and he had never expected her to reveal him standing there. The sadness in his voice touched the part of me that cared for him. Still, I mustered all the courage I could find in the fragments of me that were left behind, and with a voice that shook with tragedy, told him I never wanted to see him again.

After a few moments, I knew he had left. A cold vacant space took his place; I could feel his absence with certainty. In my mind, I couldn't recognize the voices but one or two more people spoke to me from the other side, telling me that it was okay to come out, that Diana had left on Mike's insistence. All I would say was that I wasn't coming out until everyone was gone. I stayed in the restroom until my body became numb from sitting slumped on the floor. When it was absolutely quiet,

Friendship Betrayed

I lifted myself up and pushed the garbage can away from the door. Peering out the door into the dimly-lit corridor, I knew I was alone. As I walked away, I felt the familiar silence surround me, as I stifled tears one more time.

Chapter Thirty-Three

Blaze

"Call 911! Now! Someone's car is on fire out back!" The shouts penetrated the tranquility of the morning, slicing through the quiet like a hot blade of a sword piercing my heart. I felt myself freeze in place on the kitchen floor, my gaze feverishly scanning the backyard from the vantage point of the second-floor window. A jolt of lightning hit me as I saw the vivid orange and red flames shooting skyward, the smoke engulfing the air with its menacing pillows of black. In the next second, I was running into the other room to make the call. *No dial tone! Where's my cell phone? I can't find it. Oh, my God! I've got to call...now.* Flying down the stairs, never touching a single wooden tread, I reached the phone in my downstairs office. I dialed; silence for a moment that seemed like an eternity, until the phone began to ring...and ring...and ring. Finally, a voice answers. *I'm shouting into the receiver...the address, what's happening...describing it.* I hear the question: "Is anyone in the car?" "No, but there are other cars parked right next to it and, trees...they look like they caught

Blaze

fire--the garage with stored gasoline is only two parking spots away." They've got someone on the way; another call was placed a moment before. Someone from the meeting that was being held at our center must have called amidst the chaos. The station is around the corner, literally. I'm immediately so grateful for their proximity.

I run outdoors, not caring that my unclad breasts sway under the fabric of my LL Bean nightgown. "Get away from the car in case there's an explosion!" I shriek, obediently relaying the ominous warning of the dispatcher. I'm looking for my husband, Kurt. He's calm...that's part of the beauty of this man I've married. "Are the chickens safe?" I query. *We've got a dozen baby chicks housed several yards away.* "They're in the coop, the door is closed tightly...they'll be okay", I hear Kurt speaking, slowly. His words are barely audible to me; everything seems muffled as I stand there shell-shocked, my body wracked with tremors, tears billowing from my eyes like the flow from a fire hydrant.

The fire engine arrives, although I've heard no siren amidst the swirling silence in my ravaged mind. The massive red behemoth encompasses the entire width of the driveway as it makes its way slowly into the back yard. I'm stuck in an eerie bubble of disbelief and shock, coupled with the reality unfolding before me. Friends who were at the meeting are making their best attempt to comfort me. "It's contained...the firemen are here...don't worry...the chickens are safe." *I hear them, but they don't understand the depth of what's happening.* As they speak,

Silence

I see myself wearing another nightgown, in another time and place that seems all too real. I'm in our living room on Franklin Street, sitting on a floor pillow, legs stretched out in front of me, watching the Alfred Hitchcock Hour with my mom. My long white cotton nightgown with the tiny blue flowers and ruffle around the bottom is pulled down demurely around my calves. Directly behind me, my mother sits on her big rocking chair. She leans over and chooses a section of my below-the-shoulder hair, deftly wrapping the strand around her index finger until reaching my scalp. With lightning speed and precision, she slips the hair off her finger, pulls a bobby pin from its nest between her pursed lips where it resides for easy access, and "pin curls" it expertly into place on my head. This process was repeated until no hair remained loose; a kerchief wrapped around my head signaled completion of the task at hand. I gladly endured the torture of sleeping this way to ensure the curly tendrils that would give me the Cher-like head full of hair that earned me the nickname Zapper in the latter part of twelfth grade.

My mother reminded me to please take out the garbage before heading to bed, just as the telephone rang. It was my Aunt Mary calling like clockwork to talk about the latest installment of the show we had just watched. I walked over to the kitchen sink, reached under, pulled out the small trash basket and carried it across the room to the back door. Our garbage cans were neatly stored in a small bin against the massive brick wall that ran the entire length of not only our backyard but the two houses on either side of us. The towering

Blaze

barrier was the rear boundary of the massive lumber yard that resided on the other side. Cradling the basket under one arm, I turned the knob and pushed the door open with my foot, stepping down simultaneously onto the small wooden porch. I halted abruptly, instantly losing my grip on the trash basket. Its contents flew up into the air, flying in all directions in what looked like slow-motion, as my mind reeled in horror and disbelief at the sight before me. Liquid fire billowed over the roof of the lumber yard and poured down the wall, igniting the small shed, spreading wildly across the dry grass towards the house only a few feet away. "Fire! Fire!" I shouted, feeling the velocity of my screams tear at my vocal cords. Turning, I ran back inside, slamming the door behind me. I ran to my mother, shaking her and telling her to put the phone down. She stared at me in disbelief, unmoving at first. *Save the kittens!* My mind screaming the order, I rushed into the bathroom where the eight babies were asleep in a box in our bathtub, their mother having fed them well before heading outdoors. They slept peacefully until, by the handful, I feverishly scooped them up and placed them into the fabric of my floor length nightgown, folded up around my waist as a makeshift shelter to save their lives as I headed for the front door to safety. I nearly collided with a fireman rushing up the steps to our front door. "Get my mother, get my mother out...she's right behind me," I screamed, shaking violently. Flames were licking over the roof of our house as we fled to safety across the street. The big house, having been vacated by my grandmother and my aunt and uncle much earlier, was primarily empty. Our three-room flat was

Silence

partially packed up, as my mother and I were planning to move within a few weeks, following my graduation from high school. Our neighborhood was being dismantled--house by house--to make way for a proposed highway project.

As I watch helplessly, the enormous flames before me are consuming every timber, the crackling sound of wood screaming into the night. The shattering of glass joins the cacophony, as our house disappears into the dense smoke. Endless angry bronze and ripe pomegranate flames devour the darkness of the night sky. My grandmother's pride and joy, her red rose bushes lining the front yard, turn black, then disintegrate before my eyes. The huge house is being eaten alive, as my mother, myself and a throng of neighbors watch the flames dine.

The horror of the moment expands as I shift my gaze to the two houses adjoining ours. They too have become unwilling sacrifices to the blaze. Roofs cave in, opening great gaping wounds. Their inhabitants, bodies impaled by fear and horror on the sidewalk across the street, watch homes disappear while clutching the hands of loved ones. A neighbor taps me on the shoulder and offers us a place to go, to move away from the scene that will haunt me for years to come. My mother and I follow, numbly. My footsteps feel like moving through thick mud, each footfall holding me back while I try to obediently follow my mother's voice urging me forward. The sound of the eight kittens meowing from inside the cocoon of my bedclothes, offers the reason to keep moving.

Blaze

    I vaguely remember sitting around our neighbor's kitchen table, in a dazed stupor that I assume was shock. Someone placed a blanket around my shoulders and slid a cup of tea in front of me with a few cookies. They sat there abandoned, staring up from the plate at me, as I blinked and ignored them. The scene transpiring around me felt like watching a silent movie; the others in the room were talking to my mother, but I recall no sound. I was inside a world of stillness, my entire being inert, as time passed by unaccounted for. I was catapulted back to the present at the sight of my sister, Pam, coming through the kitchen door, her familiar voice striking a chord within me. Amidst the ensuing chaos on the street, she had made her way to us – questioning anyone she recognized as to our whereabouts. Shortly before the fire broke out, she had dropped us off at home after having dinner at her house. Somewhat reluctant to bring us home that night, she had asked us to sleep over. The combination of being a school night and my mother's wanting to sleep in her own bed sealed the deal that brought us home this fateful night. Driving back to Plainville, she had arrived home shortly after the fire had begun. The niggling feeling in her gut that urged her to suggest we stay overnight had become full-fledged dread as her neighbor, Danny, banged at her back door telling her the news he had heard on his police band radio. Looking into the night sky, the inferno's signature off in the distance confirmed the grim news.

    It was decided that we would spend the night at my sister's home. Leaving our sanctuary behind, we walked into the

Silence

awaiting holocaust. The sight of our neighbor, spraying his rooftop with a garden hose in an attempt to keep burning embers from igniting, seemed almost insignificant amidst the backdrop of the firemen's apparatus discharging torrents of water into the massive conflagration that once was our home. Holding hands, single file, with my sister in the lead, we weaved our way through the throngs of people who stood transfixed, mesmerized by the dance of the flames before them. Our goal was to reach her car parked down the street behind the police barricade. My mother instinctively turned back towards me periodically, her eyes simultaneously loving and frantic as they peered out over the bandana worn to shield her asthmatic lungs from the smoke-laden air. Moving at a snail's pace, I tried to avert my eyes from the sight of the destruction that would come to be known as "The Night of Fires." I felt my mother's hand tighten around mine, as the realization sunk in that her childhood home was vanishing right before her eyes. I choked back tears, as my throat tightened and the acrid smell filled my nostrils. Even now, in this present moment, I have to stop for a few moments to breathe and relax as the all too real memory invades reality, crippling my body momentarily in response to my recollection.

In the light of the following day, my sister and I stood on the broken sidewalk in front of the devastation that remained from the night before. Charred timbers, the skeletal remains of our home, stared bleakly from the rubble. Gone were the shingles, shutters, roof, walls, floors, and doors built by my

Blaze

grandfather. A few scorched floorboards perilously balanced themselves here and there, with the melted remains that used to be our refrigerator perched upon them. The fire had gorged itself, its appetite consuming everything we owned; we escaped with the clothing on our backs and nothing more. There are no words to accurately describe the carnage, the dark void that looked like the doorway to hell. Amidst the vast emptiness, on what was left of the small front lawn sits the scorched white "clamshell" that sheltered my grandmother's Blessed Virgin Mary statue. I blink once, twice. In disbelief, I move towards the remaining stone walls surrounding the property for a closer look. The unmistakable, serene face of the Mary looks back at me as she stands, hands outstretched. Miraculously undamaged, she will later appear on the front page of the local newspaper. Standing there, transfixed, I began to disappear, sinking into that deep place inside that insulates one from thinking or feeling. Suddenly, I snap back into reality. In a moment of sheer insanity, my sister has decided to climb into the wreckage after having caught a glimpse of something that appeared to be intact, balancing precariously within reach. I grab her arm, forcing her to stop momentarily. "Nothing is worth risking getting injured," I plead. *Yet, from within the madness of seeing your home turned to mere rubble, something calls you to rescue the one last thing that may still exist amidst the apparent nothingness.* With the prowess of a mountain goat, Pam traversed the impossible, returning with a small box in her hand. She gingerly wiped the ashes and soot away with the sleeve of her shirt, revealing the familiar grey metal

Silence

container. It was mine. The heat had seared it partially closed, a gap formed at the uplifted corner disfigured by the flames. Prying it open revealed the eerie contents. When I saw what laid inside, utter disbelief fell over me like a ton of bricks. My own eyes looked back at me from the black and white Polaroid, singed only at its corners. Underneath lay the remains of an unfinished letter to my pen pal. The paper had burned, stopping just below the image emblazoned on the stationery depicting the caricature of a wooden coffin, cracked open slightly to reveal the gnarly long green fingers of its occupant attempting to lift the lid. Ominously written below it appeared the words, *just a little note to let you know I'm still alive,* and nothing more.

Chapter Thirty-Four

White Trash

One day, the powers that be in the place where I grew up decided that it would be to everyone's benefit to create a highway system designed to bring the masses to their great city. It would generate untold commerce and put New Britain on the map as a destination not to be missed. The politicians in office touted that the cost would be well worth the rewards. That is, unless you happened to live in the neighborhood that stood right in the middle of their grand design. From this perspective – our view of their grand plan – we saw things just a bit differently.

My mother had called Franklin Street her home from birth, as did the many predominantly Italian immigrant families who had settled there, bringing up their children within a strong cultural community. I too came to love this place and the people who called it home for generations. Moving into my grandmother's house at age ten, I'd spent eight years growing up in the tight-knit hamlet where everyone knew each other well enough to bring homemade soup to one another if someone was sick, or casually share a meal without making plans ahead of time. Since my mother never learned to drive, I knew how to navigate the neighborhood and its surroundings on foot. Most of our neighbors did the same or caught the bus; virtually everyone worked at the local factories or downtown stores. There is something intimate about walking the same streets every day. You learn the lay of the land, recognizing dogs and cats along the way, calling them by name. Accustomed to familiar sights and smells, a certain rhythm weaves its way into your life.

It was incomprehensible to suddenly learn that all that you held dear was to be destroyed in the name of so-called progress. Houses that nestled three generations within their walls were to be dismantled without so much as an afterthought – *unwilling victims to a wrecking ball*. When we got the news, thank God my grandmother was unaware of what was about to transpire. She now spent her days at a convalescent care facility, oblivious to the destruction that lay ahead. Rather than cause her undue despair or potentially threaten her health further, the family decided to keep up the pretense of life as usual on Franklin Street. The rest of us were left to the task of finding another place to live, packing up our belongings and saying goodbye to those we held dear.

This heart-wrenching process was halted in its tracks by the unfathomable. One evening shortly before my high school graduation, fire engulfed our home, claiming every shred of

White Trash

our existence. The flames consumed everything we owned as we watched helplessly; thankful for our lives. Shock and horror multiplied the feeling of sadness already upon us. We were not only losing our home but all that was in it – lock, stock and barrel – along with treasured keepsakes from both my mother's and my childhood.

In the aftermath that lay ahead, finding a place to call home seemed insurmountable, placing still another hardship on my mother and me. We had to find affordable housing, quite a challenge in our situation. Meanwhile, another blow had been dealt. Several days before the fire, my mother had taken out a loan for several hundred dollars to tide us over, allowing her to pay for upcoming moving expenses including deposit and first month's rent which we were bound to encounter. *What better place to keep it safe and secure other than under the mattress where she slept?* Indeed, the flames of the inferno dined extravagantly that fateful night. Unbelievably, the bank made her pay back every last cent, even though the event would be referred to as the "Night of Fires," clearly documenting the necessity to make an exception. Over the next three years, my mother paid more than interest on that loan.

Somehow in the midst of the void that became our life, my mother found a small furnished apartment close enough to New Britain High for me to walk there in a few minutes so that I could complete my last few weeks of high school. I'll never forget the look on my sister's face when we pulled up to the building. I watched numbly as the color drained from her face.

Silence

For once in her life, she was speechless. The expression on my face mirrored hers. To say the place was in disrepair would be polite, but would not come near to describing its condition. Hesitantly, we got out of the car. Pulling the key for apartment number two out of her hand-me-down black pocketbook, my mother headed for the door to our "new" house with the two of us in tow. The aged banister wobbled as my mother clutched it, the rickety wooden stairs screeching painfully under the weight of her heavyset frame as she made her way to the landing. It was the foreboding sound of things to come within. The tarnished knob jiggled under her hand as she simultaneously twisted it and pushed the creaking door open revealing the kitchen with its torn linoleum desperately trying to cover the old wooden floorboards beneath it. Inside, a small old table its laminate top stained with food rings and peppered with cigarette burns sat surrounded by four mismatched chairs in similar condition. Sharing the spotlight with rust, the chrome of the table legs was barely recognizable; clearly, its glory days were over. Directly across the room to the left was a large old sink, its faucet dripping out a slow welcoming cadence as we stood transfixed, like the three Musketeers, just inside the doorway.

    Undeterred, my mother walked around, her cane thumping on the uneven floorboards as she sized up the remaining two rooms. "Nothing a good cleaning with some Spic n' Span won't cure," she announced with a steadfast voice belying everything she'd just gone through a few days ago. Neither my sister nor myself were convinced this was possible, but set out to grab

White Trash

buckets and sponges from the trunk of her car to see if we could work a miracle.

Windows thrown open, the three of us worked for hours, the scent of pine and bleach slowly replacing the stale smell of old cigarettes. Buckets of dirty water were emptied curbside as neighbors watched in awe of the spectacle of our grand project. Finally, my mother pronounced the house clean – at least as clean as scrubbing could get the worn-out fixtures, floors, and walls desperately in need of a fresh coat of paint. Tired and needing to get home to her two children, Pam promised to check in on us the next day since we had no telephone. The reluctant look on her face said more than words ever could as she left us behind. The two of us stood side by side in the entrance, peering back at her through the torn screen on the door.

We spent the rest of the afternoon parceling out the odds n' ends donated by family and friends after the fire. Mismatched sheets covered the old mattress that we would share, while a blanket that had seen better days offered itself as a coverlet. We hung towels on a few nails on the back of the bathroom door. A bar of soap placed on a small plate on top of the toilet tank would serve both at the sink and in the barren tub devoid of shower curtain. Everything felt so foreign here; there was no joy in attempting to make this place our home. We had nothing familiar to bring us comfort, nothing we had treasured to surround ourselves with to ease the immense sense of loss

Silence

that had begun to take hold once again. A feeling of desolation enveloped me.

Dinnertime brought a bit of relief as the events of the last few days had not diminished my mother's incredible ability to cook delicious food. Once again, comfort came in the form of a good, solid meal, the familiar tastes easing the emptiness I felt inside. As night began to fall, things began to go from bad to worse. Even my mother's sunny disposition began to fade as the noisy, unfamiliar sounds of the people living in the apartments on either side of us began to filter through the thin walls. As the evening wore on, their voices became increasingly louder and more obnoxious, the result of alcohol and disagreements, the details of which we couldn't escape with no radio or television to obscure the sound. Earlier, my mother had closed the windows for a shred of privacy, locking them and pulling down the tattered yellow shades that would serve until we got some curtains. She put a kitchen chair snugly under the doorknob of both the front and rear doors once the noise level had increased. Unfortunately, it did not afford the sense of security we both longed for.

A game of rummy played on dog-eared cards served as a distraction until we were both tired enough to attempt sleep. I went into the bathroom to get ready for bed. A new toothbrush sat in a plastic cup waiting patiently. Looking into the hazy mirror that hung over the sink, the face of a stranger blankly stared back at me. She looked tired and sad, eyes weary and ringed with shadows. I didn't recognize myself. Clearly, the

White Trash

last few days had taken their toll. This was the first time I really took it all in as I shook my head in disbelief, still shell-shocked from the whole ordeal. *How could any of this be real?* A thousand questions, no good answers. My mind went blank, refusing to process anything further as I reached down to grab the toothpaste.

Climbing into bed, I laid alongside of my mother. We gave each other a comforting goodnight hug and kiss. I turned onto my side wrapping my head in the spongy pillow to silence the din. Time passed slowly as I filled my head with thoughts of graduating high school in less than two weeks. An image of my mother's face as she gave me the news that the fire had claimed yet another casualty mercilessly crept in. Somehow, she had managed to save up enough cash to buy me a class ring, destined to be my birthday present as I would turn eighteen shortly before graduation, but instead it had vanished before I ever saw it. *One more morsel consumed.* I desperately wanted to think of something else, but the devastation that overtook our lives seemed to permeate everything. Finally, the sound of my mother's snoring intruded on my thoughts. I welcomed its familiarity, letting myself be surrounded within it like a comforting womb, finally sinking into a restless sleep.

In the morning, I rose early to get ready for school. The scene of my mother already in the kitchen making breakfast created the appearance of an ordinary life. My day at school was fairly uneventful but it kept my mind focused on the tasks at hand. I considered it a blessing. Time went by much too fast

Silence

with sixth period signaling the end of the day. I dreaded going back to the apartment down the street, refusing to call it home even for a moment. Thinking of my mother waiting there was the only reason not to delay the inevitable. Alone, I walked down the sidewalk looking down at the concrete, admiring the tenacity of the weeds that poked through the cracks. A few guys I didn't recognize came up hurriedly from behind passing me by. Within earshot of their conversation as they neared the rundown building just ahead, I couldn't help but overhear the sarcasm that cut me to the core. "Let's get by this shithole before we catch something – there's nothing but white trash living here!" My pace slowed to a snail's crawl, barely moving as I watched them move farther and farther down the street. Tears welled up in my eyes as I approached the entrance to apartment two, their callous words piercing me to the core. As I climbed the stairs, I wiped them away on my sleeve banishing them instantly. Silently, I thanked God that my mother would never hear those words repeated nor feel the hurt they instilled. She had gone through enough. A smile on my face to greet her, I opened the door and called "Hi Mom, I'm home!"

Chapter Thirty-Five

David

The memories shared in these pages would be incomplete without the one long-held in my heart. My earliest recollection transports me to a moment of joyful innocence, the afternoon I met my childhood sweetheart. Pouring "tea" into his cup, I looked into eyes that recognized mine. A little four-year-old girl instantly smitten by the five-year-old David. His mother and mine sat at the kitchen table next to us enjoying a cup themselves, no doubt commenting on how cute we looked together. I remember I didn't want him to leave when his mother said it was time to go, yet off he went. Luckily for me, he lived five doors away, so we were destined to grow up together. I can honestly say that as we grew older, our connection strengthened, and my heart became more filled with love for him. As you read this book, you will find him here and there within its pages. He popped in and out of my life in much the same way. For me, relationships are the threads that create the tapestries of our life. David, my first love, will be forever interwoven in the fabric of mine.

Silence

I learned early on that great love comes from being open to both give and receive. We also become vulnerable to feeling its loss. Leaving David behind when we moved from the projects broke my heart. I would only see him occasionally afterward when his mom would visit mine and bring him along. Outside of sending him an occasional letter, he disappeared from my life at about age twelve, re-emerging at around age fifteen. Through all that time, David held the key to my heart. My girlfriend Janie endured countless stories about him. Since we were both fairly shy and didn't have any real boyfriends, Janie was eager to meet him to authenticate his existence. We concocted a plan based on the premise of visiting the projects to show her where I grew up. I knew he still lived there because our mothers had kept in touch over the years.

Deciding the element of surprise was a good idea, one Saturday afternoon we made the hour-long hike and knocked on his door unannounced. After a few minutes of waiting, no one had answered the door. I remember looking at Janie and thinking maybe this wasn't such a good idea after all. I had mustered up as much courage as I had to make it this far, but it quickly dissipated on those porch steps. Just as we were about to turn away, the door opened. There he stood a fifteen-year-old god, more gorgeous than I remembered. Those unmistakable sky-blue eyes looked out through the screen door. Meeting his glance, I immediately melted like ice cream on a hot day. "Uh, hi," was all I could manage to say. He kept looking directly at me; now I was a fish wriggling on the end of a hook. I

David

swallowed hard. "Do you remember me?" I dared to say, the words hanging suspended in the air. Tilting his head slightly to one side, his long dirty blond hair slid across his forehead spilling onto his shoulder. Janie released a single sigh. Without a doubt, the boy on the other side of the door was not only real, he was magnificent.

"Hey, Deb, what are you doing here?" the low provocative whisper came. I was not prepared for this. He had grown up into someone I would never dream to approach. His looks were killer, reminiscent of Brad Pitt in *Legends of the Fall*. Stunned, I realized he actually recognized me. "Just decided to visit the old neighborhood and thought I'd see if you were home," I replied, praying he'd play along and not laugh out loud at the obvious. As Janie and I stood transfixed on the porch, David threw his hair back like a beautiful horse tossing its mane. Never once shifting his gaze, it seemed like an eternity passed as he considered his next move, and responded, "Well, I am -- now what?" His voice was an invitation, as a smile began to curl the corner of his lips. "Who's that at the door?" came a girl's voice from over his shoulder. "Ah, geez," his sister blurted out as she rolled her eyes and smirked, recognizing me. "Let's take a walk," David said, choosing to evade his sister rather than wait for my reply.

In sync, the two of us backed down the stairs to give him room to open the door. Luckily, we didn't trip over each other as he stepped out in his full glory. Somehow, I managed to remember to introduce him to Janie as we followed him like

Silence

hungry cats across the street towards the old playground of our youth. Sensing my discomfort, David let me off the hook. He said he thought it was pretty cool that we had shown up out of nowhere. We hung out in the pavilion for a while, talking about nothing in particular. I remember being amazed at how easily we connected after so long. He had plans with a friend soon, so our visit was short-lived. Nonetheless, it was long enough to give Janie and I plenty to talk about on the way home and for hours afterward. Much to my surprise, the visit laid the groundwork for us to keep in touch now and again, mainly via telephone.

David and I shared the same birth month although he was a year older. Once he turned sixteen and able to drive, his friend Paul and he decided to reciprocate our earlier visit. Unlike us, they did not show up unannounced, so I had the chance to call Janie to plan. My sister had set us up with a cool room in her basement to hang out. I remember the two of us waiting nervously for them to arrive, rearranging the chips, dip, and soda over and over again to get everything perfect. We were so distracted that they caught us off guard coming down the cellar stairs behind us. Janie did a double-take when Paul appeared just behind David. I could read her mind in an instant. It was love at first sight. Here we were, nervous plain jane types who had hardly ever talked to guys, hanging out with two that any girl would die for. Luckily, Paul was very easy going and talkative, breaking the ice for the group. David portrayed more of the quiet rebel, as he had since we first met. It was the

David

very trait that drew me to him like a moth to a flame. When he spoke, there was something meaningful to it, at least to me. The two of them were planning to start a band and eager to share the details. Janie and I sat enraptured listening to every detail with awe.

As it turned out, David was destined to be the lead singer. I was to be on the receiving end of a serenade I'll never forget. While babysitting for Janie's younger brother, we decided to call the boys after settling him in to watch television. Halfway up the stairs I sat, telephone cord pulled as far as it would go in an attempt for a little privacy. When the phone rang, David answered. We shared small talk for a moment. As the conversation progressed, I asked him how the band was going. He responded by singing *a capella* to an audience of one. The instant his first words reached my ears, my heart began to melt. "Unchained Melody" drifted languidly over the line. David's voice filled my entire being, each syllable leaving me breathless – I damn near fell off the edge of the stairs. I held the receiver out momentarily so Janie could hear the reason behind the dazed look I knew was on my face. The last words David sang, *Godspeed your love to me*, were followed by absolute quiet. Neither of us uttered a single word. A nudge to my shoulder from Janie prompted me to speak. "Wow, I had no idea you could sing so well," was all I could think to say. My heart said he sang it for me; my mind uttered not a chance. This single sentence would come to define our non-consummated relationship. The uncertainty that had become so commonplace

Silence

in my psyche undermined my ability to truly embrace the depth of the feelings we had for one another. I felt safe and content the way things were, not fulling realizing that I was playing dodgeball with his feelings as well as my own.

A span of another two years would come between us. Janie and I began to drift apart as we shifted from junior to high school. I spent most of my time studying rather than on extracurricular events. Never to be one of the cool kids, I was not included in any of the cliques with the other girls. Instead, I kept to myself with a few friends who had also been left behind.

The butterfly finally emerged from its cocoon the second half of twelfth grade, after a few of the more non-conformist girls befriended me. Much to the dismay of my stenography teacher who had been grooming me for business success, I shed my neat, pulled-back hair and nondescript clothing for a new look. In 1971, for the first time ever, seniors were allowed to wear jeans to school. Unlike what kids today wear, we wouldn't have been caught dead in worn or ripped denim. Patty, my newly found friend and mentor, gave me a pair of her size six jeans and a very fitted dark blue Henley long sleeved shirt to make my debut. I was introduced to makeup and shown how to use eye shadow and mascara. What a difference! She had also worked on my hair over the weekend, trying out a new style with her curling iron. The result was a head full of long tendrils spiraling down my back. The transformation was so complete that when I walked into school Monday morning with my newly found posse, all heads turned, but no one recognized

David

me. Taking my usual seat in English class, Mr. Montgomery took one look at me and asked, "What happened, young lady, did you put your hand in an electrical socket?" Without thought or hesitation, my response escaped my lips. "No, sir, to get this look I had to put both hands in!" I couldn't believe what I had just said to a teacher, and expected the worst, especially from the notoriously moody Mr. Montgomery. Instead, he promptly christened me "Zapper" and called me by that moniker for the rest of the year. The name stuck. So began my life out of the cocoon, albeit surrounded by a very small circle of friends.

Graduation was upon us within a few short months later. I faced it with a mixed bag of trepidation and excitement. My life was in a total state of flux after losing our home in the fire described elsewhere in these pages. There was a big party being held to celebrate which Patty wouldn't let me miss. I had nothing suitable to wear, literally. Patty's cousin Cathy surprised me with a dress she had made for me. I'll never forget what it looked like. Long and fitted, it tied around the neck, leaving my shoulders and back bare. Its deep purple background with small dark-colored orchids scattered on the fabric made it striking. She had created the most beautiful dress I had ever owned. When I put it on and emerged as *Zapper*, I actually felt attractive – a new experience for me, indeed.

There was some Boone's Farm apple wine being passed around the party. I poured a glass, hoping it would help me feel less self-conscious and uptight. While the dress was great, I had underestimated how odd I would feel in something so risqué

Silence

compared to my usual clothing. As I stood in the far corner of the basement with the half-empty glass in my hand, movement in the hatchway caught my eye. Clad in black jeans, t-shirt and boots, he moved like a panther coming down the steps in search of his prey. Long sun-kissed dirty blond hair framed his tanned face, aviator frames hiding his identity from everyone but me. For a moment, time paused, the girls' stares locked on their faces. I couldn't move, as one deliberate step after another, he came straight towards me. The panther stopped too close for comfort. I didn't utter a sound. "You don't know who I am, do you?" came the provocation. "Yes, I do." "Then tell me my name." As he spoke, his head tilted just the way I remembered. Every cell in my body knew his identity. Somehow I still had to be certain before I gave him his answer. Close enough to touch his face, I reached up with both hands and slid the aviators down just enough to peer over them into those deep pools of blue I knew would be waiting. Then, in an effort to regain the little composure I had left, I pushed them slowly back into place. Almost inaudibly, I gave him his answer: "Hello, David."

We moved to a quiet space behind the stairs to talk. As he slid the sunglasses onto his head; those baby blues of his immediately worked their magic. Our conversation startled me. A few months earlier, his mom had passed away. Because I had never been comfortable with attending wakes, my mother had gone to pay her respects to her old friend alone. Now, his eyes beginning to pool slightly, he asked why I hadn't attended the service. *I always knew he was close to his mother; so then why*

David

wouldn't I know that he needed to see me, talk to me? I blinked back a few tears of my own as he spoke these words; and, I instinctively hugged him. Whispering in his ear that I honestly didn't know it mattered so much, I let him feel how sorry I was to have hurt him. Stepping back, it dawned on me that I had never touched him so intimately before. Taking the glass from my hand, he took a sip and then placed it to my lips. "It's okay now," was all he said, taking my hand and leading me out the same way he had arrived.

The night air cleared my head and put me back in my body. I asked what brought him to this party since he did not go to the same school and had graduated a year ahead of me. The answer was simple and to the point. He had a feeling I'd be here and he wanted to see me. Considering we hadn't spoken for so long, this was amazing, yet, on the other hand, it felt completely logical to me. We walked over to a Harley Davidson parked farther down the driveway; it was his. There was no one else around. Again, those beautiful eyes of his locked onto mine. He spoke quietly yet his words pierced the stillness: "You know how I've felt about you all these years and I know you feel the same. You can't deny it." I stood there stunned by his words, as he continued on. "We've always cared about each other; maybe now that we're older we should finally do something about it. Why don't you come with me, and we'll go someplace where we can be together?" His voice was strong and sincere. There was no doubt in my mind that he meant what he was saying because my heart was pounding out the same message, silently.

Silence

Looking into his eyes, feeling the depth of his feelings – I froze. I was scared out of my wits by two things -- being alone with him since I'd never even kissed a guy; and, secondly, I was petrified of motorcycles. Embarrassed to confess to either, I made some stupid excuse about having to stay at the party with my friends. For what felt like eternity, we stood face to face with no further words exchanged. Finally, he turned and got on the Harley, not looking back as he drove off. Numb, I stood in place listening as the sound of the engine faded into the distance. I called out for him to stop and come back, regretting my decision. As tears filled my eyes, I realized it had been a silent cry heard only by my heart. I stood alone looking into the night sky; the stillness was absolute. David was gone.

Time passed and I didn't hear from him again. He never knew how much I regretted not being able to tell him the truth. I was so naïve and uncertain of my own budding sexuality and overwhelmed by the potency of his. Two hearts had been broken that night – of that, I have no doubt.

Life went on and the wallflower finally blossomed. I had married shortly before I turned twenty-one, giving birth to my first daughter at twenty-three. I had never forgotten David; yet, over time I learned that love has many faces, and the heart has room for all we love.

One day, out of the blue, thoughts of David woke from their dormancy. I felt a tug at my soul, a feeling that it was important that I reach out to him, although I didn't know why.

David

As a married woman, it didn't feel like the right thing to do, although my motives were entirely innocent. I chose to ignore the continued urging I felt from deep within. Not to be denied, instead the communication came in the form of a dream. I had jolted awake in my bed during the night while dreaming of David. In the morning, I felt unsteady. A sense of foreboding permeated the day. The dream turned into a nightmare when I learned that his life had ended that very night. A cold veil of sadness descended over me. I read his obituary over and over again, disbelieving. I would never have the opportunity to reach out to him now. It was too late. Tears lodged behind my eyes, held at bay by my need to keep silent. Young and inexperienced, I didn't know how to explain my complicated mix of feelings to the husband I loved.

Summoning courage from the depths of my soul, I knew what needed to be done. As I climbed the stairs of the funeral home, the cold of winter chilled me to the bone. Accompanied by my mother, I attended his wake. After paying her respects, she left me alone by his side to say goodbye in silence. I could feel his presence; he knew I was there for him this time.

The tapestry of my life is made of many threads – undeniably, David wove his magic into its creation. I smile knowing his spirit lives on – there is more to weave.

Chapter Thirty-Six

The Chameleon

This chapter has been gnawing at me since I awoke this morning. There has been an incessant barrage of words, thoughts, and emotions running through my mind continually; and, so I am sitting down to put them on paper. It feels important to me that this book needs to have a portrait of my brother Victor, referred to by most as Junior, amongst its pages. Not one painted solely by the stories about things that happened between us when I was a young child, but one that reflects the many facets of the man. It's no easy task. As I look back from the vantage point of the experience of age, it's clear to tell he wore many faces. My early childhood memories of our relationship were a blur; vague, odd flashes of images here and there that never came together as a whole. It wasn't until in my early forties, as I began my formal training in the field of energy healing, that the pieces came together. The deep process of self-discovery brought with it long hidden memories of abuse suffered at his hands; events that my child's mind buried to

The Chameleon

afford me the ability to cope with life lived with a brother defined technically as a psychopath.

Nowadays, my life's work is being a holistic practitioner, guiding people through the process of healing their emotional wounds. This book is helping me testify to the fact that one can heal the deepest of hurts through the act of self-forgiveness. True forgiveness freely given allows a wound to heal. Compassion infuses the wrong with understanding and love that dissolves the energy of the act itself. It is turned inwards so that the pain can be released, no longer keeping you a prisoner of the misdeeds of another. The perpetrator's hold cannot exist in this state of grace. It does not erase the wrong or hurt, but it will heal you deep within your soul. It is from this place that I share with you a portrait of my brother, *the chameleon.*

Looking back over the years, I'd say I've never encountered anyone who could be so many people without manifesting multiple personality disorder. To call him a genius would be accurate, as his intellect always appeared leaps and bounds above others. His schemes were epic – planned from every angle and missing nothing. Junior could be an engaging conversationalist, pondering the philosophies of Nietzsche for hours. His comprehension of the works of Carlos Castaneda left me both mesmerized and confused as a young teenager trying to understand these conversations. Deeply intrigued by the mystical, he instinctively knew of my innate intuitive nature long before it blossomed, often remarking that I would understand these two philosophers and more than I could fathom someday.

To give him accolades as an actor would be appropriate. He was charming – I remember when there would be three women sitting on the sofa all waiting for him to come home and see who would have his affection for the evening. Strangely enough, none of them seemed to be jealous of the other. Apparently enamored with the same man, they would all describe him differently if asked. No doubt he knew how to play his part with each one of them, giving them what they needed. While I was never privy to the details, somehow I believe he was the total "ladies man," always knowing how to show whomever caught his eye "a good time." Somehow, he obviously satisfied them enough to keep them coming back for more.

His "charm" worked wonders with more than women. Junior had a notorious reputation for being a con artist; ostensibly, it was well earned. My brother spent many of his adult years defying the establishment's rules to say the least. Much of his life from his mid-twenties on was spent in and out of prison; his "alleged" crimes ran the gamut from petty to bank robbery. I use the term in deference to my brother, as he always maintained his innocence even with the most clear-cut evidence in tow. I'm certain, given his ability to talk himself out of uneasy situations, he more than likely got away with a significant amount of transgressions of the law.

The Chameleon

Despite his many faces, there was a distinct element of commonality that ran through the ever-changing landscape of my brother's persona – meticulousness. I can't recall a time when I saw him looking disheveled in any way. Always well put together, his clothing while not expensive was well cared for. I remember how he would use yards and yards of masking tape on a makeshift roller made from discarded toilet paper innards, painstakingly removing any trace of cat hair or lint from his trousers. The components of his wardrobe consisted primarily of black clothing chosen to showcase his trim muscular body, silhouetting his physique. Although short in stature at five-seven, his presence commanded the attention of a much larger individual.

My brother's hair was both his mane of pride and the bane of his existence. Junior never left the house with a strand of hair out of place. The finished style left no clue to the time consumed to produce the look itself. Due to its coarse, wiry nature coaxing his hair into the short-cropped duck bill design of the day took Junior a minimum of twenty minutes. The regimen included pomade, Aqua Net hairspray, and a barrage of choice swear words until he would emerge from the bathroom satisfied.

In his day, sneakers were worn by guys who played basketball, not as everyday footwear. You never saw them on his feet; I daresay he didn't have a single pair. He did, however, own two pairs of black leather lace-up shoes which he cared for in impeccable fashion. The routine never changed. Junior would

Silence

cover the floor with newspaper, reverently placing his large container of Kiwi paste formula, matches, a small container filled with water, cloths for applying and removing the polish, and a soft brush upon the paper. It was a mesmerizing process. I would watch him strike a match, holding it under the metal container of polish until the contents began to melt slightly. Wrapping his index and third fingers in a clean soft cloth, he'd dip into the warmed polish, retrieving just the right amount of paste. Touching it to the waiting leather, his fingers deftly swirled it clockwise in small circles spreading it evenly across the surface of each shoe until he was satisfied with the coverage. A clean cloth replaced the first; as the removal process began with the same due diligence as the application. Next came the ceremonial sprinkling of a few drops of water across the tip, letting them slither off the side as a new dry cloth began to buff the finish. Junior's shoes got the best treatment – a "spit" shine albeit water replacing spittle. The entire procedure was repeated three times before he would even consider the next step. I'd wait patiently for the sound of bristles touching leather, as the brush slid rhythmically across each shoe signaling the final step. With each pass, the shine became more and more pronounced until it replicated the surface of a mirror reflecting my brother's pleased countenance back at him.

Junior loved music, mainly Motown; and, dancing. He emulated the moves of James Brown – practicing "splits" until he could do them with ease. Friday nights were always spent with the ladies at the Rumpus Room, a local dance club in the

The Chameleon

60's. My great love of soul music came from hours of listening to The Temptations, Isley Brothers, Four Tops and so many other great artists. Compelled to learn the lyrics, he'd play the 45's over and over again – picking up the tone arm gently and putting the stylus back down with the patience of a saint – diligently writing down each phrase with care. I attribute my ability to identify songs from the first beat or two from listening along with him for hours, sometimes being "in charge" of restarting songs while he wrote.

As I recount these good memories of my brother, it's still hard at times to fathom that there was such a distorted other side to his personality. Even I, bearing the brunt of much of his sadistic tendencies in my early years, still connected with the part of him that could make me feel at ease; even to the point of laughter. The explanation, while no great consolation, lies in the definition of the traits of the psychopath: *anti-social personality disorder, oftentimes criminal; highly intelligent, skilled at manipulating others – charming their way through life; obsessively meticulous, calm and fearless.* And, last but not least *a wolf in sheep's clothing.* Ironically, one of his favorite songs was "Little Red Riding Hood" by Sam the Sham & the Pharaohs.

Junior finally "hit the wall" sometime in the late 80's. Suffice to say that after breaking out of jail somewhere – the exact location I can't recall – he went entirely too far in a rampage that landed him in a forensic institute for the criminally insane. I visited him there a few times; it always felt odd

Silence

and disconnected due to the extreme safety precautions they undertook with inmates and their visitors. Visitors were required to leave all personal belongings like pocketbooks in a locked cubicle; belts had to be removed as well as any type of jewelry. Then came a "pat-down." It felt degrading somehow, albeit understandable from their perspective. I was simply there to visit my brother, but this cold ritual left me on edge. Initially, Junior still appeared to be himself. There was a "cool" about him that gave him the appearance of being in control – even in confinement. Nevertheless, there is a banality in a prison that creeps into those that inhabit it. As time passed, Junior became more edgy than cool – he began to disappear into the walls that surrounded him. A certain look might catch my eye that made him feel like my brother again; other times the distance created by his environment created an odd chasm between us. After enduring the stress of numerous visits, I chose to stay in touch by writing rather than experiencing the strain of seeing him in person. This was a difficult decision as my brother had burned a lot of bridges during the last few years, so I had become his "lifeline to the outside".

Junior became obsessed with playing the lotto. He spent his free time "figuring out the system" and enlisted me to buy the tickets for him. Accompanying his lengthy letters would be a few dollars, along with a specific list of numbers to play and when. This was serious business for him and he would regularly call to remind me to get them. I kept up with buying his tickets for months, despite my strong adversity to gambling.

The Chameleon

After all, it was a pastime that connected him with the outside and some type of normalcy, I supposed. Then, one day, I opted not to buy the tickets. It just went against my grain to gamble, and I finally had enough of it. In that fateful moment, things were about to change in a way I would never have surmised. Dave, my partner at the time, came home that evening with the news that my brother's numbers had finally hit it BIG. It felt as if the life was draining out of me, as I told Dave that I didn't play them that night. I watched his face turn pale white in response. We both knew that Junior was going to call any minute excited beyond measure – from his perspective he had hit the jackpot. Dave thought there was only one way to handle it and that was to go along with it. After all, I was supposed to be the caretaker of the money on Junior's behalf until he got out – so chances were with the length of this sentence, he'd never know what really happened. Well, that's not how I played it. The phone rang; I answered. Following in the honorable footsteps of George Washington, I couldn't tell a lie. Junior thought I was kidding; I assured him I wasn't. The deafening echo of a telephone receiver slamming on its cradle confirmed he believed me. A while later, he called back...sounding more subdued this time. He said everything was okay with the caveat that I would have to promise never to miss buying another ticket. That wasn't an option for me anymore. I had made a choice to honor my own feelings first, something very rare for me at the time. The audible "click" on the other end of the line signaled the conversation was over. Several days later, a terse letter found its way to my mailbox. There was no salutation

Silence

inside, merely a handwritten message stating that he no longer wanted to have any connection to me whatsoever; that I was not to attempt contact with him in any way, shape or form ever again. For all intent and purposes, he no longer acknowledged me as his sister. It was unsigned.

There was to be no contact between the two of us for the last ten years or so of his life. He spent his days within the walls of the formidable prison – one that no doubt catapulted him into oblivion. My brother died in a fortress of his own making – allegedly from heart failure. He was 54 years of age.

I cast his cremated remains into a beautiful waterfall deep within the silence of the woodlands, one of the few places where he always found peace. As the water carried him away giving him his everlasting freedom, I read aloud the poem I wrote for him.

Released

Throughout the years
you dwelled mainly within yourself
amidst shadows
on the fringes of a world unknown by most
touching only occasionally
those you left outside your walls.
Yet, I can recall times when we walked side-by-side
you talking, me listening
while you regaled tales of the world

The Chameleon

from a perspective most of us
would never encounter.
I reaped awareness
I would never have known
without you in my life.
I question not why your path followed
the rocky road it did
trusting that it served its intended purpose.
And, now in Spirit
I know we will travel together again
into realms we couldn't reach before
with love and knowledge lighting the way.

Chapter Thirty-Seven

The Saint

All along, one of the biggest roadblocks I've encountered in remembering the sobering memories of my childhood has been why no one ever stopped the abuse I suffered at the hands of my brother. Ever ready to absorb responsibility, I let myself believe it was because no one knew what was happening. Even as I write this, I am sugarcoating the real question that makes its home in the deep recesses of my psyche. I've always colored the tale with the idea that my mother could not have known about my brother's behavior or else she would have put an end to it. After all, my mother was a saint. Growing up in the projects, as they were called back then, my mother was the one everyone would come to for advice on just about anything from remedies to take for an upset stomach to how to heal a broken heart. I remember sharing meals with neighbors when they didn't have the wherewithal to afford food. There was always room at Connie's table – no questions asked. Everyone knew her as someone you could always count

The Saint

on to listen to your story, and you knew she could keep your secrets too.

Knowing all this, how on earth could I give any amount of credence to that unnerving feeling that would gnaw at me whenever I would dare entertain the thought that my mother knew anything about what was transpiring between my brother and me? On top of it all, my mother and I were always tremendously close. My father was pretty much out of my life in my formative years, as my mother and he stopped living together when I was about eight. With my siblings so much older than myself, I spent much of my time with my mother. As I grew up, I spent more time with her than I did with friends. So, there was no other conclusion for me to come to when I asked myself "the" question, other than that my mother just didn't know what was happening to me because, being the defender of the downtrodden that she was, *of course she would have stopped my brother in his tracks.*

Over time, I found I no longer asked myself that question. That is, until one afternoon when Kurt and I were visiting two of our very dear friends, Suri and Jade. After having a delicious lunch together, we made ourselves comfortable with a cup of tea in front of a roaring fire. Conversation flowed easily as it does amongst friends. One thing led to another and, as the conversation deepened, the subject of my writing this book became the topic. I shared my bewilderment about being unable to find the motivation to continue writing. I prattled on with reasons that began to sound more and more like excuses.

Silence

I honestly wanted to get to the bottom of things, but I just couldn't connect with the process. Somehow, deep from within my subconscious, the answer arose. In a voice choked with emotion it poured out of me. *I was afraid that there was no value in the story I had to share and that no one would listen.* It was just that simple. The room suddenly disappeared and I sat there frozen in another time and space, the words I had just spoken reverberating in my ears. I was brought back to the present moment feeling the warmth of Jade's hand on my knee as she knelt by my side. My frightened eyes met the clear blue of hers, and with strength and clarity her heart-spoken words penetrated the void. With a fierce certainty she told me that I needed to tell my story because it was desperately needed. My words would be not only heard but would reach out to those lost in the same isolation. There would be many who would benefit from knowing what I had experienced. My experience reflected their own. I could feel the hot tears beginning to fall down my face as my rational mind loosened its grip of fear and my very soul recognized the truth in her words.

Without hesitation, Suri seized the momentum of this realization and asked the big question, "Why did I believe that no one would find any value in what I had to say?" The voice that answered was that of an injured, insecure little girl. *Suddenly, I had become the frightened child who felt she had no value because no one had found her worthwhile enough to save.* In the same breath I excused my mother from this equation saying she was the exception because she didn't know what was

The Saint

going on. The very instant I spoke these words, the knowing in Suri's eyes connected with mine confirming the scariest secret locked away in my heart. I found myself shaking my head as I trembled, acknowledging out loud that my mother knew of my brother's propensity towards malevolence, but had put the pieces together too late. I cried in earnest now, every tear held back in stony silence pouring out of me.

As my tears subsided, I embraced the outpouring of love and acceptance that I felt. The child within me had needed to speak aloud her deepest fear to break the bond of silence. I knew deep within that there were no boundaries to the love I felt for my mother. A child's confusion was replaced by a grown woman's understanding. I could feel my eyes shine with the light of this recognition dissolving the remnants of my fear, opening the gateway to my heart. There would be more for me to learn, another awakening about our relationship to come.

Chapter Thirty-Eight

Safe Harbor

Uncontrollable tears are running down my face as I write these words. One of the biggest moments of realization I've had while undertaking the venture of birthing this book just crashed down on me like a ton of bricks. I often have to work through an impasse when I talk about my mother, especially when I mention something that feels even remotely derogatory. *She was overprotective of me. Her fear of my being injured in some way, shape or form kept me from learning to swim or ride a bike. There. I said it. It hurts to say it. She did her best. She was alone except for me. My siblings were much older than me. I was good company – she kept me close.* All true in some manner of speaking. Where's the big epiphany in all that? The reason, the answer behind the silent, unanswered question.

She knew. She knew. She knew. Figured it all out about my brother's abuse somewhere along the line. Never said a word. Like daughter, like mother. Silently weaving a safe cocoon where I could nestle in and grow up. Keep me close, keep me

Safe Harbor

safe. Wounded herself by the knowledge of my suffering, she would do whatever it took to keep anything else from happening to me again. Too late to keep the misdeeds from occurring, prevention was now the key to creating a safe harbor for her precious cargo – me.

The ghosts of the unanswered questions have always haunted me: *Did my mother know? If she did, why didn't she do something about it?* I had settled on the answer that made the most sense. My silence kept it from her – from anyone. Junior had made me an offer I couldn't refuse. Releasing a nasty looking spider from its glass prison, a mason jar, he had instructed me to watch closely. The spider, sensing its new found freedom, moved across the floor at lightning speed – stopping on a dime as it sensed its proximity to the baseboard. Then, with the ease of a practiced master, it slid itself effortlessly under the almost invisible crack between the linoleum and the wall. "Did you see that, how easily the spider got inside?" came my brother's question, delivered with a sinister grin across his face. "If you tell anybody about what I do to you, I'll do something worse. One night when you go to bed, you'll feel something crawling up your leg under the covers – something I left there waiting for you. Remember… it can get inside your little girl parts even with your underpants on – just like you saw it crawl under the wall. So, don't say a word and you won't have to worry. Always remember, I'll know if you do, and momma can't protect you all the time."

Fear bought my silence. My mother chose hers. I understand.

Chapter Thirty-Nine

Vertigo

Spinning – slowly at first, vague, almost imperceptible. Gnawing at the edges of my consciousness, the uneasiness in my stomach, wavering back-and-forth, uncertain as to the path it wants to take. *Balance...balance. Stay steady, it will pass. Breathe...breathe. Feel your body fill with life-sustaining air.* Try as I might, my attempt is feeble at best. The spinning heightens suddenly; the room spins before me. I feel like I am on one of those amusement park rides that swing you around endlessly – faster and faster, uncontrollably. Closing my eyes brings the now full-blown nausea onto the blank canvas I've created in mind. I swallow again and again in an attempt to push the wave down. I'm succumbing quickly; standing feels foreign, a massive feat I cannot accomplish. I reach for the countertop in front of me, I beg for the steadiness it offers. Convincing myself it will hold me upright, I feel my heartbeat, I hear it in my ears, it's everywhere. *Wait...wait, breathe, hold on; it will pass momentarily, as it has before.* Eons of time pass by, drowning me in a sea of disconnection; I'm floating

Vertigo

away through the void of uncertainty. *Hang on, something is changing.* I feel the gentle tug of being pulled back into the moment. The brakes are on, the crazy ride is slowing down, it will be over soon. The dizziness begins to recede as the end draws near. The surreal landscape under my feet is giving way to terra firma. Shaky, I'm back in the kitchen and, thankfully, there is the familiar stillness. Inanimate objects do not move but stand, like silent sentinels, where they belong.

Two days ago, laying on a gurney at the local emergency room, I was being treated for these "symptoms," coupled with a headache that felt like it was exerting enough pressure to split my skull apart. The afternoon before I felt "off," like part of myself was missing and I was walking around looking for it. I went to bed early to sleep it off, relegating it to the sudden heat wave that doused us with 90-degree heat plus massive humidity – not a combination I do well with under any circumstances. My slumber was disturbed by repetitive images nagging at me mercilessly from the edges of the dream world. I couldn't seem to wake up, but I wasn't truly certain I was sleeping at all. My body felt like a hot air balloon floating away yet being held back by one remaining strap, only haphazardly tethered to the ground. Waking to the headache, I went downstairs and curled up on the couch. My cat, Koko, ambled over; her blue eyes reflecting compassion. Petting her relaxed me; she gazed up at me, knowing the steadiness of her purr was working its magic. Still, things did not improve, the pressure in my head would not relent. Coupled with the dizziness and nausea, Kurt

Silence

and I decided a trip to the walk-in clinic was required. After the exam, the doctor prescribed going to the emergency room for a thorough workup. Not exactly where I wanted to go, yet the need to stop the pain overrode any doubt about its inevitability.

It's early in the day, so the emergency room is fairly quiet. I'm pretty much the main event, except for the sound of a woman's voice screaming vague obscenities from across the room. I overhear that she's coming down from some drugs; I'm relieved she isn't dying. The questions I answered earlier at the clinic are repeated, except there are steps to be taken in response. There will be a CTSCAN to eliminate the possibility of a bleed in my brain; such a thing is apparently a consideration with sudden onset and the continued display I exhibit. Deep inside, I know that it will show this is not the case; but am willing to dissuade any fear of its potential. I'm returned to the room; a bag of saline is hung to nourish my body, as dehydration may be the main culprit. There's an IV in my arm, into which a nurse injects a needle full of a drug to stop the headache; then another to quell the nausea. Because they pulse into my bloodstream immediately, it is blissfully only a short while until both conditions subside. My eyes become heavy, I'm finding it impossible to stay awake, the drugs and my exhaustion work in unison to put me to sleep. Startled, I wake at the sound of a foreign voice asking me how I am while simultaneously introducing himself. I manage a hello, and am told by the doctor that my CTSCAN was negative, with no abnormalities indicated. While not quite certain why all this occurred, a

Vertigo

problem in my brain is not the culprit. Relief is apparent in both mine and the doctor's expression. Ninety minutes later the saline bag has been sucked dry, and I'm feeling tired but much better. I can be discharged to go home with the instructions to follow-up with my physician, and told that I should not hesitate to come back if the whole thing starts up again. A prescription is part of my discharge paperwork, one that should quell any recurrence.

It's now 48 hours post episode and I'm having Sunday breakfast with my husband, Kurt. We are talking about the emotions behind illness, something that I truly believe is key to why something occurs and how to heal it. After all, this is what my life's work is all about. I'm drawn to write this book as a testament to how our emotions, felt or forgotten, can shape our lives. The conversation is brought up as I've had a slight, brief recurrence of vertigo this morning after being out in the heat. Delving into what an episode feels like brings up an old memory of a hard-to-describe feeling I recall having as a young child. My best attempt is to relate it to a feeling of falling backwards into a tunnel full of something akin to a dark night sky filled with bursts of starlight. All the while a loud sound resembling the beat of my heart coupled with a dense heaviness would come over me. It was scary when it began, but as I succumbed to it, familiarity replaced fear. I don't know where I went, but it felt safe somehow. As I write these words to describe it, I am gifted with a feeling of knowledge that I am on the right track, remembering on a much deeper level. I see a safety valve releasing in response to an overload of pressure in the form of fear. It is the life-saving mechanism of a child's mind and body under siege. The removal of conscious thought and presence in a circumstance so threatening that my sanity is saved by the gift of it disappearing into the unconscious. Lack of awareness shelters me from events beyond my comprehension.

The process of writing this book entails remembering long-forgotten, buried memories. Raking layers of debris laid in place as protection years ago is simultaneously stirring up both an emotional and physical response within me. Spared from these feelings as a child, I am literally conscious of the emotions that were withheld long ago. Part of me knows that the experience is cleansing and healing; the other dreads it happening. *My vertigo is a fight between recollection and forgetting.* This is the catalyst that will allow me to acknowledge and release the emotion. I am in the present, a place where I have the wherewithal to mend the tears in my psyche. *Acknowledging the emotional detoxification taking place, I have reclaimed my voice to tell my story – to be heard – to come out of the silence of my stronghold – to heal completely at long last.*

The hot tears flowing from my eyes cleanse my heart and soul. My mind's eye reflects a child who feels whole for the first time ever. At last, I've found me.

Epilogue

For much of my life whenever I would become sick I would get laryngitis, sometimes losing my voice for days on end. As I became older, stress would induce the same throat problems. It was so commonplace for me that I really stopped giving it a second thought. Everything changed when I began to delve into the healing arts and personal process work that would lead me down the road to becoming an energy medicine practitioner in my early 40's. Becoming aware of the human energy field and the chakra system opened my eyes to the cause behind dis-ease. I questioned why my throat chakra appeared to be the main recipient of the manifestation of illness. The connection became increasingly obvious as time passed – it is the gateway to expressing your authentic self through communication.

As I began to work energetically to release the blocks in this area, painful memories began to emerge. Parts of my childhood that had not only been dormant but of which I had no recollection began to come to the surface to be revealed. I had always been very quiet and low key as a child and teenager, feeling more comfortable alone or in the limited company of other "outsiders". I was always an easy mark for those wishing to ridicule rather than befriend. Fortunately, this neither stopped me from being creative nor did it curb my love of learning. It did, however, stop me from giving voice to my opinions unless I was standing up for a fellow downtrodden individual.

When the sleeping memories of abuse woke up inside me, they did so in an onslaught. Suddenly, I became aware that the power of my freedom of speech had been repressed by the fear instilled deep within me as a child. It was time for me to restore my voice, to take my place as the healer I was meant to become. In order to meet my full potential, I needed every part of me intact. The emotional wounds that had festered for so long needed to be tended to. In the process of working energetically to accomplish this I learned so much. The hunger within me to not only reclaim my own voice but to be of service to others could no longer be abated.

From my perspective, emotions are akin to our life blood. When they are out of balance, we become out of sync – unable to clearly express our potential. In clearing away the emotional debris caused by the abuse and ridicule I experienced as a child, I began to reclaim my voice. As a healer, it grew stronger as I was able to affirm my beliefs and express who I am more fully. I accepted my originality rather than seeing myself as an outsider, and moved beyond the limitations imposed by others that I had wrongly accepted as my truth.

In the past twenty years of my life, my healing practice has grown exponentially. Embracing the knowledge that emotions affect our ability to heal our bodies, I laid the groundwork to begin to observe what I call our inner landscape. Doing so affords us the opportunity to better understand how the experiences of our lives deposit layers of emotions deep with us. We oftentimes either consciously or unconsciously bury them much to our detriment. This knowledge led me to develop a step-by-step process of clearing the layers of energetic debris caused by these imbalances. Emotional Archaeology[SM] is all about discovering your hidden treasures, the strengths held deep within your soul – by clearing away the debris that keeps you from experiencing your true nature. My impetus to create this modality came from my own healing journey.

Writing *Silence,* I've come full circle – I'm now able to openly acknowledge my boundless potential. Mine is a labor of love, a reflection of my dedication to my practice as a healer to embrace my commitment to help others heal the wounds that keep them from knowing and trusting themselves fully. To stand vulnerable – in the light not in the darkness – and share my story has given me peace and a greater understanding of myself and those who share the path of my life. From within the silence these stories are shared openly in the fervent hope that you, too, will strive to reclaim the power and strength of your own signature sound–your voice.

It is time to raise our voices in unison – our vibration will be felt and the sound heard throughout time.

Deborah Ravenwood, EMP

Afterword

Resilient is the first word that comes to mind when I think of my mother. Her silence cost the innocence of her childhood, but her inner strength preserved the child within so that she could eventually speak. She has given voice to her history, and in turn gifted many others, myself included, with a road map towards wholeness reclaimed.

Our family bears the legacy of our collaborative struggles and paths taken through the pain and sadness to claim ourselves. Some have taken a heartbreaking turn for the worse along the way. Others have forged a stronger sense of self and mission; the past a piece of what propels us forward to offer a gentle hand or a listening ear to travelers drawn towards us. My maternal grandmother was the one whom the neighborhood women would flock to for a treat and some understanding words. My mother is a healer, a writer, and a life coach, supporting others through her strength and connection with spirit. I am a mental health clinician, working in schools to provide play, expressive art, and sand tray therapy to children and adolescents who have experienced trauma, anxiety, depression, and other struggles in their childhood. My sister found inner strength and courage she didn't know she had when diagnosed with breast cancer. She chose the road less traveled healing herself using holistic methods; and, now shares the knowledge and experience she has gained with others, shining the light on alternatives to traditional therapy. We each have found our unique routes towards healing others.

This book is the tie that binds us all together, woven through the fabric of my mother's past, present, and future.

Having spent the summer simultaneously reading this book and working with my clients, both children and families, I am struck by the similarities in the stories I have read and the stories I have heard. My mother is breaking the silence of painful experiences lived through long ago, and yet these type of traumatic instances still occur today. The difference is in the silence. When my mother was a little girl, child protective agencies, reporting laws, research and discussions about sexual abuse were largely nonexistent. It was not until the child abuse prevention laws began to be put in place in the 1970's that the necessary societal changes began to occur. Mandated reporter laws currently require health care workers, school personnel, mental health professionals, child care providers, and law enforcement officers to report child maltreatment; and, thus children have more eyes on them, offering protection and safety from abusers.

Nevertheless, child abuse continues to be a problem that escapes even these proactive measures, as the amount of fear, shame, and secrecy perpetuates the silence that surrounds both victims and perpetrators. The cycle of abuse is a tough one to break. Many perpetrators were once the ones victimized, and many families who keep silent have a history of abuse in their families. When I do an intake to begin individual therapy for a child, I often meet with the parent first in order to have space to ask sensitive questions and gather a trauma history from them before meeting with their child. It is not unusual to have parents reveal to me that there is a history of abuse in their family; and, often the parents have also been victims of child abuse as well.

It is heartbreaking work, and yet it is a labor of love. I cannot go back in time and stop my uncle from behaving the way he did towards my mother, nor can I lift the veil to see what the roots of his cruel behaviors were in his own life. I can, however, be present to the children and families that come to me for help, and do my best each day to listen to their stories and teach them how to both protect themselves in the future and heal from the traumas of their past. My mother continues her work as a healer, transforming her painful experiences into the alchemy of Emotional Archaeology[SM], breaking her silence and enabling others to do so as well. My grandmother may have held her silence until her last breath, but she was also the vessel that held the painful words others spoke to her when they knew no one else dared to listen.

You, too, have accomplished something meaningful just by reading this book. You have allowed my mother's voice to be heard. Take her words with you. If someone trusts you with their story – whether their voice is strong or wavering – their face young or old, listen to them. Hear their words. Trust that you will be making a difference by your very act of being there for them. If you are the one who has been touched to the core by my mother's words, let them encourage you to find your voice and your path to healing. The path may be bumpy, tangled with roots and dark along the way, but trust in yourself and you will find your light.

Kymberli Anne Ravenwood Goldsmith, M.A., LMHC

About the Author

Silence is the first book to be written by Deborah Ravenwood, although others will follow including one concerning her personal life coaching practice, Emotional Archaeology[SM] to be released in 2017. She believes that finding the key to a well-balanced life gives you a greater sense of yourself by healing the wounds that keep you from knowing and trusting yourself fully. Deborah is passionate about empowering people to move through life embracing the realization of what they are truly capable of being and becoming. For over twenty years, Deborah has helped people move through the challenges in their lives with grace. Through non-judgmental listening, Deborah creates an opening for you to find your voice.

Deborah's clients have called her a "gifted, caring spiritual energy healer" and have sought after her guidance for many years. In praise of her work, clients often comment that she has taught them to believe in themselves by realizing the treasures they hold within. Deborah's deep sense of compassion and intuitive sense provides a nurturing environment for her clients to experience an enhanced level of wellness.

Together, she and her husband, Kurt, created Ravenwood Holistic Wellness Center – as a peaceful place to discover health and harmony in your life. They are stewards of the land at Ravenwood, both living and working on the premises. Their commitment to each other is strong and grounded in Spirit. Enthusiastic about helping people to reach their optimum level of health in a nurturing environment, they focus their intention on the highest good for each individual. You are invited to visit the author's website at www.deborahravenwood.com